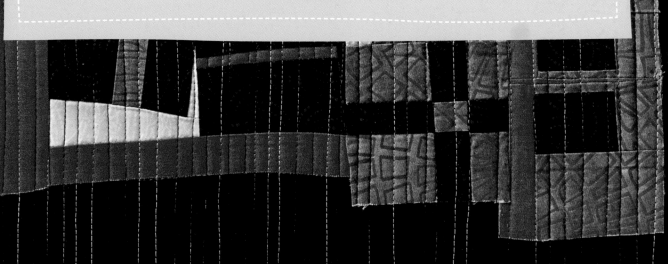

create your own
improv quilts

MODERN QUILTING
WITH NO RULES & NO RULERS

RAYNA GILLMAN

C&T PUBLISHING

Text and photography copyright © 2017 by Rayna Gillman

Photography and artwork copyright © 2017 by C&T Publishing, Inc.

Publisher: Amy Marson

Creative Director: Gailen Runge

Editor: Lynn Koolish

Technical Editor: Linda Johnson

Cover/Book Designer: April Mostek

Production Coordinator: Zinnia Heinzmann

Production Editor: Alice Mace Nakanishi

Illustrator: Linda Johnson

Photo Assistant: Mai Yong Vang

Style photography by Lucy Glover and instructional photography by
Diane Pedersen of C&T Publishing, Inc., unless otherwise noted

Published by C&T Publishing, Inc., P.O. Box 1456, Lafayette, CA 94549

Library of Congress Cataloging-in-Publication Data

Names: Gillman, Rayna, 1941- author.

Title: Create your own improv quilts : modern quilting with no rules
& no rulers / Rayna Gillman.

Description: Lafayette, CA : C&T Publishing, Inc., 2017.

Identifiers: LCCN 2017027676 | ISBN 9781617454448 (soft cover)

Subjects: LCSH: Patchwork--Patterns. | Quilting--Patterns.

Classification: LCC TT835 .G575 2017 | DDC 746.46--dc23

LC record available at https://lccn.loc.gov/2017027676

Printed in the USA

10 9 8 7 6 5 4 3 2 1

CONTENTS

DEDICATION

To the North Jersey Modern Quilt Guild and especially to Aleeda Crawley, who cofounded this warm, friendly, diverse, inclusive guild with me in 2012. We encourage personal expression and diversity of size, shape, and purpose in our quilts, including art quilts for the wall. Machine piecing, hand piecing and/or quilting, and fusing all work for us. We love solids, but we also love combining them with contemporary or vintage fabrics, hand prints, and hand dyes. Perhaps we should call it "postmodern."

This book reflects the vision we had for the NJMQG, which is still strong and growing five years later. Thank you, Aleeda.

ACKNOWLEDGMENTS

First, huge thanks and hugs to Lynn Koolish, my patient and good-humored editor. Your flexibility has made this book possible. Couldn't have done it without you. Really! And many thanks to everyone at C&T who worked with me to edit and design this beautiful book.

I'm also grateful to the following companies:

Michael Miller Fabrics, which supplied me with many of the luscious Cotton Couture fabrics.

Hoffman Fabrics, whose Me and You collection of modern batiks added great accents.

P&B Textiles, whose Urban Scandinavian fabrics added pizzazz to my quilts.

Superior Threads, for the variegated King Tut and Bottom Line threads.

The Warm Company, Fairfield Industries, and Quilters Dream, which sent batting for my quilts.

FOREWORD

This has been a labor of both love and insanity. The love part was having an idea and doing the writing. The insanity was starting a book before I had a single quilt to show as an example.

Because I am so visual, it was impossible for me to write about the process without having first made the piece. This meant I had to experiment as I went along, discover what worked and what didn't, make a quilt, and then write. This took more time than I had anticipated, but it was an exciting voyage of many trials, errors, and successes.

Some of the "what if?" experiments worked, and you see them here. Many of them sparked new or alternate ideas I did not have time to follow up with; there are some pictures of those, still on the design wall. Still others will be cut up and made into new free-form modern quilts, and they may appear on my blog someday.

If writing this book has confirmed anything, it is that for me, visualizing how something should look when it is done is a recipe for failure. I can only work with freedom and creativity by experimenting, without trying to imagine to how it will look at the end. I highly recommend that you try this freeing approach: Leave yourself open to serendipity and your creativity will soar.

I encourage you to use this book as an idea generator, not as a recipe book. If you engage with the process, the result will take care of itself. Enjoy the love and the insanity on these pages, and let them be the sparks that get you started.

Affectionately,

—*Rayna*

INTRODUCTION: A SMALL SLICE OF (MY QUILTING) HISTORY

One of the things that drew me to modern quilting was the term *improvisational piecing*. I have been working this way since the late 1990s, teaching hundreds of students to let go of their rulers and cut freehand.

Of course, when I learned to make a quilt in 1974, there were no rotary cutters, so we used rulers to trace the pattern pieces on the back of the fabric and cut them out with—*gasp!*—scissors. Edges cut with scissors aren't necessarily perfectly even or straight, so the teacher—who came from a long line of scissor-wielding, quiltmaking ancestors—said, "Don't worry if the seams don't match. Fudge it and do the best you can." Since I had flunked seventh grade sewing, these words were music to my ears. And I discovered, in fact, that nobody but the "Quilt Police" noticed or cared whether the piecing was perfect.

Around 1996, I ditched the patterns and the ruler (except for trimming edges or cutting geometric shapes). Little did I know that the Whitney Museum Gee's Bend exhibit in 2003 would usher in a new era of what I was already doing: wonky, improv, original work. And happily, improvisational piecing is part of the modern aesthetic—along with some other terms that describe my philosophy.

- No rules
- No borders
- Freedom in how to construct quilts
- Personal expression

Since that is the way I have been working for two decades (Someone said to me recently, "You were modern before there was modern."), I knew it was right up my alley in a lot of respects.

As the modern quilt movement has matured, I am seeing more and more quilts made from patterns, a reminder of the books from more than 40 years ago when I began to quilt. Modern quilt books and magazines, full of detailed instructions on yardage, cutting, and block placement have proliferated. This is a *good* thing for the thousands of new quilters who have discovered a new way to express themselves with an old art form.

But just as many of us have evolved from following patterns to making original quilts without a pattern, so I expect that many of you who use patterns to make your modern quilts are, or will soon be, tempted to break out and experiment.

This book offers you a way to make your own personality shine through in your modern quilts as you explore working without a pattern. As you work your way through this book, remember that everything you do can lead you in a direction that is truly your own!

HOW TO USE THIS BOOK

Everything old is new again, but with a twist. Solids and negative space reminiscent of Amish quilts still look fresh today with the use of white or gray backgrounds. Old-fashioned, traditional patterns emerge in larger scale; new settings; and bright, lively fabrics, which often come from one designer's collection.

Whether you have been making traditional quilts and want to break out a bit, or have already jumped feetfirst into the modern movement, you can use this book as a starting point for making original quilts with a modern appeal.

You won't find patterns here—you'll find possibilities. Starting with simple shapes, you'll see how to create modern quilts in your own individual style. You'll see ideas and examples you can use as inspiration for no-pattern, one-of-a-kind modern quilts. You select the colors and fabrics, you choose the scale of the units or blocks, and you make the changes you want to make as you work on your design wall.

While some consider modern quilts to be utilitarian, I believe the modern aesthetic works beautifully as art for the wall. So I encourage you to experiment with small pieces. When you work small, you have the opportunity to try different settings, fabrics, and designs without using a lot of fabric. And if you want to make a bed quilt, you will already have your smaller piece to serve as inspiration.

If you've read my other books (*Create Your Own Hand-Printed Cloth* and *Create Your Own Free-Form Quilts*, both from C&T Publishing), you know that there are no mistakes. If you don't love something, you can always recut and reuse it, add or subtract from it, or turn it upside down. And you can still keep the modern aesthetic (or not), as you choose. No need to worry about what's modern and what's not, or whether you consider yourself a modern quilter. Join the party and come along!

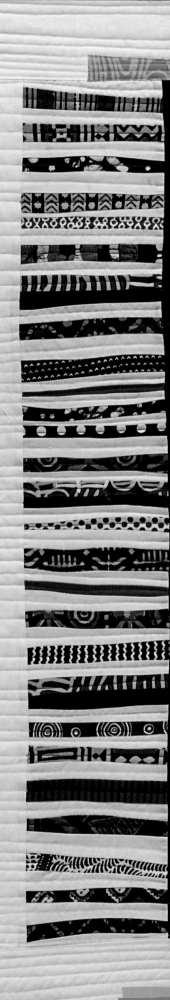

Mid-century design, which originally inspired the look of modern quilts, is generally defined as clean and spare, with straight lines and extensive use of black, white, and neutrals with accents of pure color.

As the modern quilt movement has evolved, so has the definition of modern quilts. It now includes an expanded palette, and the terms *graphic prints* and *low volume fabrics* have been added to the modern quilt vocabulary, as substitutes for *bold* or *high contrast* and *light* or *low contrast*. Since anything printed is graphic, and low volume makes me think of turning down the sound, I'll stick with bold or high contrast and light or low contrast.

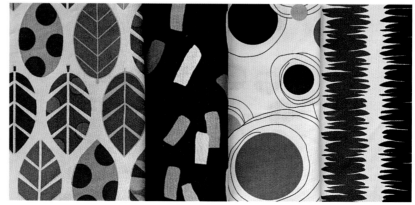

Bold or high-contrast prints

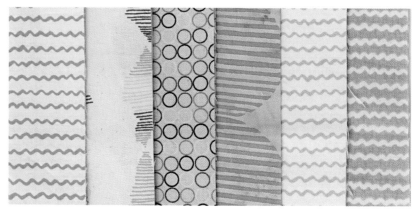

Light or low-contrast prints

If you're not sure about low contrast, look at your fabrics in black and white.

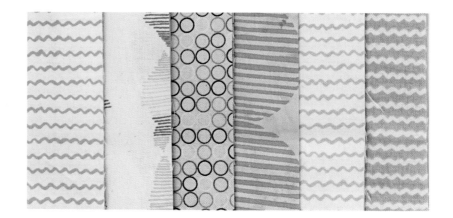

EVERYTHING OLD IS NEW AGAIN

Many of today's modern light prints can read as solids; some have a quiet or small print, and others are reminiscent of old-fashioned fabrics from a century or two ago. In fact, the images of these updated quiet prints sent me scurrying to my trunk to pull out a nineteenth-century Log Cabin and some antique blocks that were made with charming small prints barely distinguishable from some of today's modern fabrics.

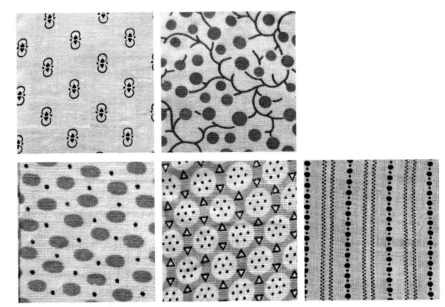

Nineteenth-century small prints

Vintage fabric

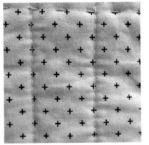

Modern repro fabric

Vintage fabrics

Modern repro fabric

Nineteenth-century
Log Cabin

MODERN QUILTS WITH REPRO PRINTS

The challenge to making a quilt with small, light prints is to keep it from being bland. For this, you need to add a spark here and there of something unexpected—something bright or in a different scale. As in life, variety adds spice. Combine your light, quiet, small-scale prints with a few larger-scale prints and stronger colors to make the piece shine.

Svetlana Sotak's large-scale handwriting print, high-contrast stripes, and touch of red ignite small sparks in her improvised, mostly neutral quilt. The candy-stripe binding adds humor to the piece and is similar to the stripe in the vintage Log Cabin block (page 9).

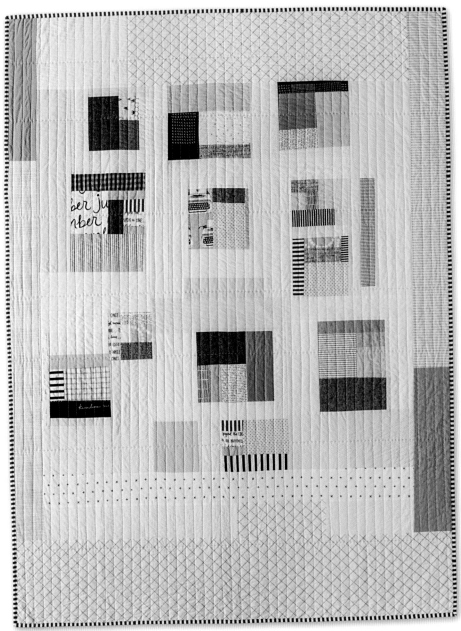

Untitled by Svetlana Sotak, 51″ × 68″, 2015

MODERN QUILTS WITH RECYCLED FABRICS

Cindy Anderson's modern quilt emerged from a pile of outdated traditional blocks she knew she would never use as they were. Instead, she cut some of them up and set them into a white background, where they became small gems in a modern setting.

In Motion
by Cindy Anderson,
20˝ × 30˝, 2015

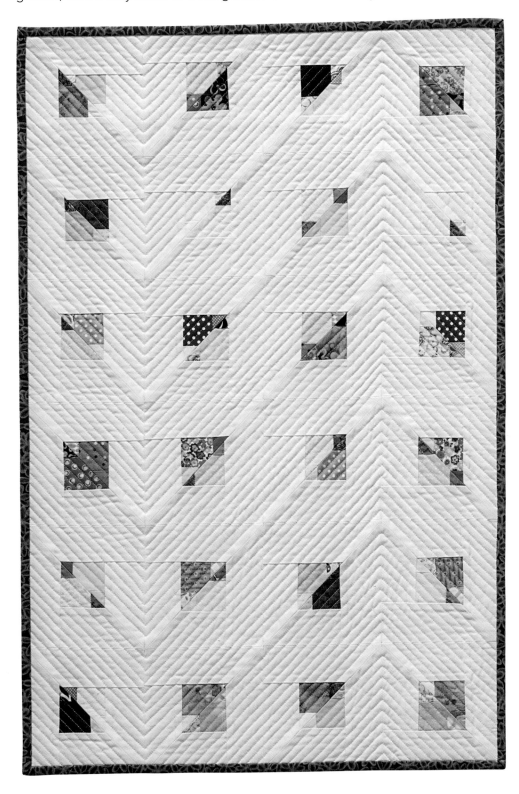

Inspired by Cindy's use of old fabrics and repurposed blocks, I opened the bags of scraps my grandmother had brought home when she worked in a factory, sewing pajamas and housedresses. It gave me great joy to combine her mid-century stripes and seersuckers with today's solids and a gray hand-dyed background.

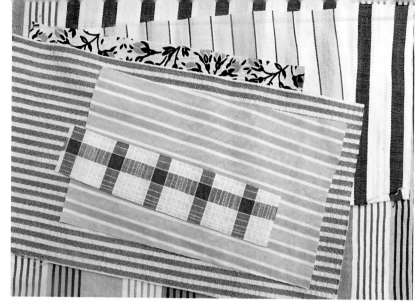

1950s fabrics

Photo by Rayna Gillman

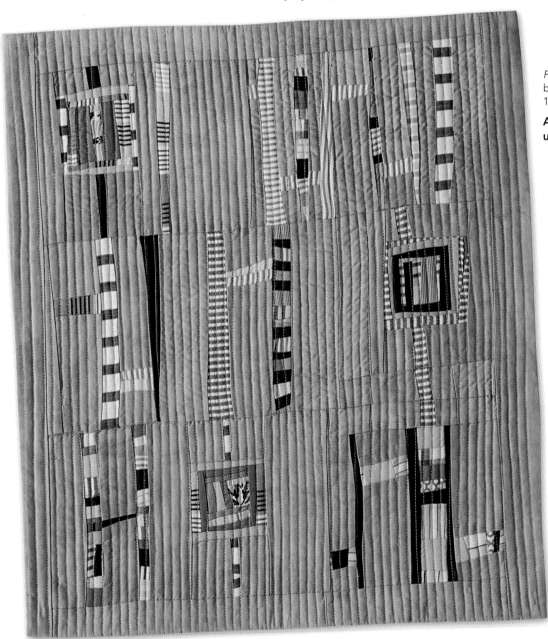

Pajama Game
by Rayna Gillman,
13″ × 17″, 2016

A modern quilt using 1950s fabrics

WHAT ABOUT BATIKS?

You may have read, as I have, that "batiks are not modern fabrics" and are not to be used in modern quilts. This is opinion, not law. If vintage fabric and its modern incarnations can be used in modern quilts, why can't batiks?

Batik is not a category; it is the process of dyeing fabric with a wax resist. There are modern fabrics made with this process, and they are high-contrast enough to work well. But most typical commercial batiks are a challenge to use effectively because they are primarily medium-value fabrics. Modern likes contrast, and the batiks you are used to seeing tend to "mush" together. If you look at a group together in gray scale, you can see how close the values are. It is often hard to distinguish them from one another if you use several together.

These pastels may appear light, but they are really light mediums.

Although these colors differ, the values are very close when they are viewed in black and white.

Even the lightest commercial batiks are medium lights and the darkest are medium darks. If you want to use them in your modern quilt, check the values (see Step 2: Check the Values, page 19) with your smartphone or your computer. Then audition them in small bits with high-contrast prints. See if they work for you.

ethnic batiks

Nonetheless, if you love batiks, take heart! There are lively, bold African, Indian, and Malaysian batiks that will add excitement and variety to your modern quilt. You can find these and other splendid ethnic prints in fabric shops or online (see Resources, page 95). They are a way for you to individualize your quilts, and they mix beautifully with solids and modern prints.

African and Indian batiks

West African, South African, and Aboriginal prints

MODERN ETHNIC

Marimba evolved from strips of ethnic batiks, modern prints, and a few solids. The busy African, Indian, Aboriginal, and modern fabrics work together because the design is simple and minimal, the palette is limited, and there is a lot of white space.

Because of the fabric choices, this piece has an international feel. It would be equally striking in solids. In fact, a year after I made this quilt I came across a photo of a West African weaving that included this motif—in solid black on ecru. There is nothing new under the sun.

Marimba by Rayna Gillman, 22″ × 40″, 2016

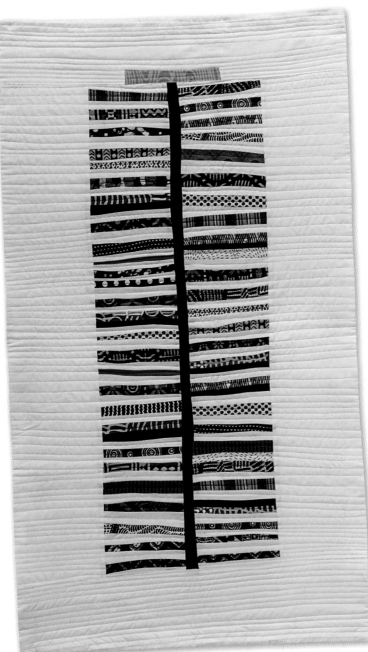

BE FLEXIBLE WITH FABRIC CHOICES

There is no reason to restrict yourself to only "modern" fabrics, so consider mixing them with others that strike your fancy. In the right proportions and values, almost anything can go into your modern quilt. As you know, fabric choices can make all the difference in what a quilt "says."

It's fun to experiment with one motif (not necessarily triangles, of course) and a range of fabrics.

Compare these two pairs of triangles.

The first two are made with muslin and African batiks.

The second pair is made with modern prints and solids— same motif, different mood.

- -

ADD TO YOUR STASH

In addition to ethnic fabrics, modern prints, and solids, consider using the following:

Vintage fabric   Look through thrift stores and estate sales for fabrics that may be 20, 50, or 100 years old but still look fresh. Mix them with new fabrics and repurpose them in a modern setting.

Hand-dyed fabric   Try hand dyes in place of solids. Or you may have some shibori in your stash. These fabrics can add extra depth and interest.

Hand-printed fabric   You may have printed your own fabrics or bought some hand-printed fabrics. Audition these with solids and see how they work together. Once you cut something into small pieces, it looks totally different (and often better).

The improvisational, scrappy, modern aesthetic has room for all kinds of fabric choices, and this is where the fun and creativity come in. Put your imprint on your quilts: Use a wide variety of fabrics and combine them in a modern way!

IS IT MODERN OR ART? BLURRING THE LINES

Although the modern quilt movement began with a focus on making utilitarian quilts inspired by mid-century design, modern quilters have begun to expand their repertoires. They are making "modern traditionalist" quilts; using paper-piecing patterns; and working in palettes that go beyond the mid-century solid black, white, gray, and bits of color. They have also begun to make "minis," or quilts for the wall, as art quilters have done for decades.

Since art quilts are made to be displayed, not used, there has begun to be an overlap in these two formerly distinct areas. Many art quilts contain some or all of the features defined as modern: geometric designs, improvisational piecing, minimalism, negative space, and solid fabrics. Does this make them modern?

Some people use the word *contemporary* to refer to art quilts. Contemporary means "belonging to the present," so the word applies to anything current, no matter how you define it. Can there be modern art quilts? Are all modern quilts art? And does it matter? Trying to categorize today's quilts is futile because so many straddle the boundaries.

START SIMPLE

Since one of the tenets of modern quiltmaking is simplicity—simple design, a minimalist aesthetic, and a clean look—we are going to start with a fresh, clean approach. Later, you'll see additional modern looks, but for now, wipe the proverbial slate clean and get into a modern frame of mind.

CLEAR THE DECKS

Give yourself room to play by putting away anything extraneous. To begin, all you need on your table are some solid fabrics, a cutting mat, a rotary cutter, and, yes, a ruler. I choose to use the ruler sparingly, but more on that later.

You'll also need a design wall. If you don't have one, tape a large piece (36″ × 48″) of 100% cotton batting to a wall with blue painter's tape or cover a bulletin board.

Finally, make sure you have a digital camera or use your smartphone/tablet so you can take pictures as you go along—this is important!

START WITH SOLIDS

Because many modern quilts use solids and because solids allow you to see color and value without being distracted by pattern, we're going to start our journey with them. Select a pile of solid or hand-dyed fabrics in a variety of colors and values, including black and white. It's a good idea to check the values by taking a photo and converting it to black and white or by using a value filter to make sure you have a good range, including dark mediums and light mediums.

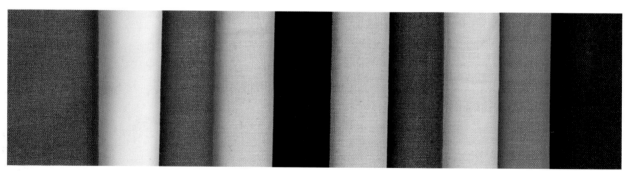

Warm and cool colors

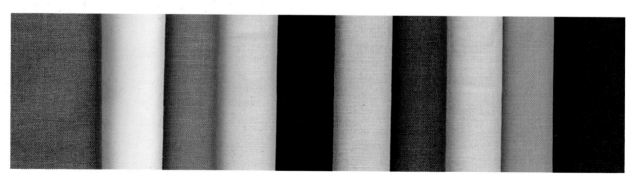

A black-and-white photo shows the range of values.

SELECT THREE COLORS

To keep it simple, begin by working with three solid colors: a dark, a medium, and a light. Since one of the hallmarks of a modern quilt is the frequent use of neutrals, start by selecting fabrics in black, white, and a third color you love in a medium tone. If you have a smartphone, use the camera's black-and-white setting to check the medium value. Modern quilts are not confined to solids, but for now, solid fabrics will keep things simple and minimalist, while the high contrast of black and white will allow you to see the design possibilities clearly.

USE ONE GEOMETRIC SHAPE

You may be surprised how much variation there can be in only one shape. In the next chapter, you will experiment with one shape, and you'll see the possibilities of using it to create a modern quilt without a pattern.

CONSIDER THE RECTANGLE

WHY THE RECTANGLE?

Why the rectangle? Because it can't get any simpler than that, because there's something elegant about the shape, and because the rectangle is more versatile than you might imagine.

When you visualize a rectangle, you normally picture two longer and two shorter sides. Let's say the length of a rectangle is roughly twice the width and call it the classic rectangle.

A classic rectangle

A square is a rectangle with four equal sides—let's call it a fat rectangle.

And a strip, of course, is a skinny rectangle whose width is a mere fraction of the length.

A skinny rectangle

As it turns out, you'll use all three of these rectangle shapes as you create your improv quilts.

A fat rectangle

ONE SHAPE, INFINITE VARIETY

You'll see how versatile the rectangle can be and how you can create something simple, original, and modern by experimenting. In this chapter the examples are small, but you can change the scale and work much larger if you choose.

note

Full disclosure: When I began this chapter, I had no idea where this was going; I just improvised as I explored. It was a voyage of discovery for me, using the words "what if?" Ask yourself the same thing and let this be a voyage of discovery for you, too.

EXPLORE THE POSSIBILITIES

Let's explore the versatility of the rectangle by starting with intent and improvising along the way. Begin with a basic inventory of classic and skinny rectangles and go from there, slicing up the common shapes and creating new units that can become a modern mini. I'll show you some of my improv results, but your results can (and probably should) be vastly different as you play with the shapes and your rotary cutter.

Start with about ½ yard of each fabric in case you decide to make more units later for a larger quilt. Right now, you are working toward a modern mini—a good size for experimenting.

1 *Start with black, white, and a medium-value color.*

Black and white give you automatic neutrals and provide high contrast. Now it's up to you to pick a medium-value color that makes you smile. (Mine is lime green.)

2 *Check the values.*

Compare your medium color to the black and white to make sure the values work. The best way to do this is to take a photo of all three fabrics together and turn it into black and white on your camera, tablet, or smartphone. Compared to the black, the lime green looks light, but the black-and-white photo shows the light green as a medium. You can use a light medium to dark medium; either will work, as long as there is good contrast with both the black and the white fabrics.

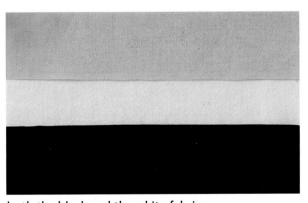

Lime green provides good contrast with both the black and the white fabrics.

3 *Pick up your ruler.*

Yes, you are going to cut the rectangles with a ruler. While I don't advocate cutting everything with a straight edge, this is one of the times I encourage it. But don't worry; you'll soon put the ruler down again.

4 *Cut the rectangles.*

Cut 4 rectangles about 4″ × 6″ from each color, for a total of 12 rectangles: 4 each of black, white, and your medium color.

5 *Slice off a strip from the long edge of the rectangle.*

Using the ruler, slice a 1″ piece from the long edge of each rectangle, for a total of 12 rectangles 3″ × 6″ and 12 strips 1″ × 6″. This will give you enough to play with as you begin. You may decide to add more later on if you want to make a larger piece.

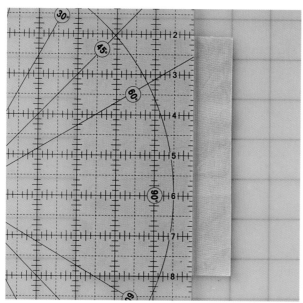

Slice a strip off each rectangle.

6 *Slice through the center and insert a strip.*

Cut each rectangle in half lengthwise and insert a strip of a different color. There are 2 methods you can use, which will give slightly different results.

Method 1: Cutting with a Ruler

If you want to start from a more structured base, cut each rectangle exactly in half using a ruler.

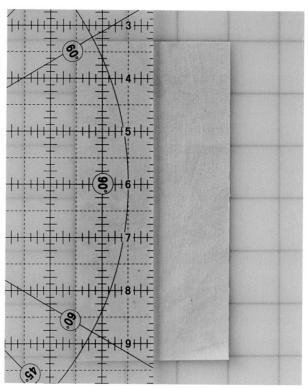

Cut the rectangles exactly in half lengthwise.

Insert a 1″ strip into the center using a ¼″ seam allowance. This will give all the pieced rectangles a uniform look.

Strip sewn in with a ¼″ seam allowance

For a more improvisational look, cutting without a ruler results in natural variations.

1. Place a ruler with the edge in the middle of the block (1½˝). Place a 1˝ strip along the edge of the ruler.

2. Remove the ruler and slice just inside the edge of the strip. You will have a gently curved edge.

Cutting freehand

3. Place the pieces right sides together and sew. Repeat with the other side to insert the strip.

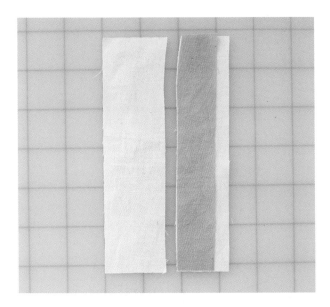

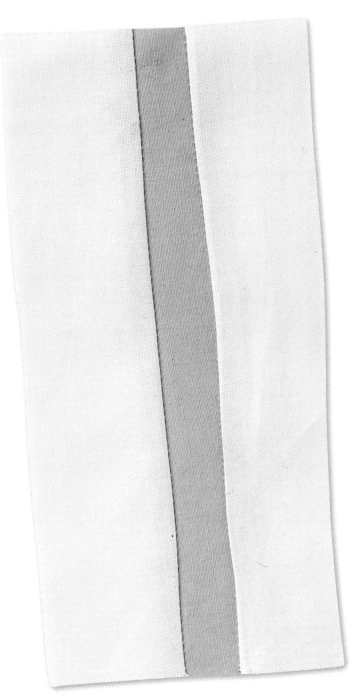

Inserted strip

Do this with all the rectangles until you have used all the combinations and have 2 of each combination, or 12 rectangles all together. No matter what you use as your medium color, when you line up the rectangles they will look very graphic. But as you will see as you proceed to explore the possibilities, they will not all remain intact.

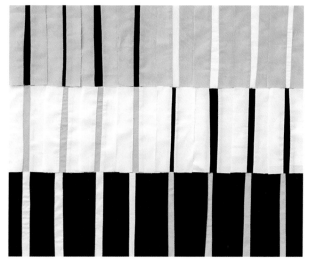

Four of each color combination provides enough units to make a larger piece or a series of smaller ones.

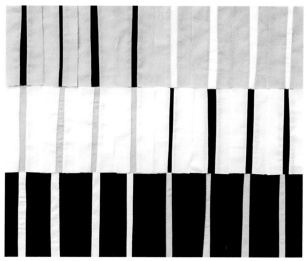

Wouldn't the photo in gray scale make a stunning piece in neutrals?

TIP: If you want a more improv feeling, vary the seam allowances a bit as you sew the strips.

"WHAT IF ... ?"

Now comes the part where you ask yourself the million-dollar question and start experimenting to find out the answer. Here are some of the questions you can ask yourself as you work with your rectangles.

What if I put one rectangle of each combination in a column and set the columns in rows on a neutral ground?

Before you make more rectangles, get an idea of what this will look like by copying and pasting a photo of the pieced rectangle onto a blank page to see how it will look. Try some different combinations while you're at it.

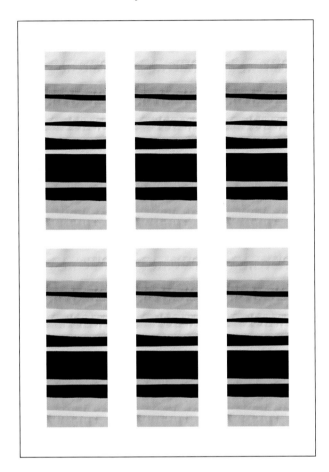

This option would make a very simple, graphic modern quilt. But since the first idea is rarely the best, you'll want to explore more options, as I did.

What if you sliced some 3″ × 6″ rectangles in half crosswise and made 3″ × 3″ squares?

What if you cut a few in half again to create 1½″ × 3″ rectangles?

What if you added 2 of these small rectangles to each side of the larger ones?

You can play with possible arrangements.

How would it look if you removed a row of the small rectangles?

And then, *what if you worked in only two colors?*

Now you would be playing with positive/negative space—one of the defining components of many modern quilts. But you wouldn't have gotten there without all those what-ifs.

I followed that "what if?" route, and before I knew it a high-contrast, graphic quilt had evolved, seemingly by itself.

In Sequence by Rayna Gillman, 25½˝ × 32˝, 2016

CREATE YOUR OWN IMPROV QUILTS

FEASTING ON LEFTOVERS

Whether you're cooking or quilting, you're bound to have some extra ingredients on hand when you are finished. And when you improvise, one thing invariably leads to another. These leftover scraps were simply begging to be used somewhere.

When you have leftovers, sew them together into units, as I did with these bits. Then put them into a "future quilts" box.

Leftovers for future use

Sometimes you won't have to wait for the future to use your scraps. As I was organizing the scraps from this chapter, I picked up a leftover green unit and placed it on a solid black rectangle. The green squares floated!

Then I placed the black unit with the green line on the same background.

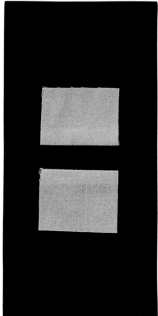

Leftover units in green and black

The positive-negative effect works well in any color combination, as long as there is contrast.

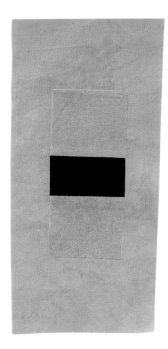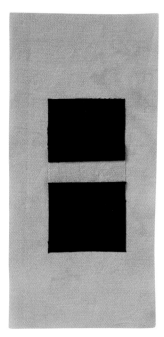

Wow! It's a whole different look and another version of positive/negative. I played with all three colors in their variations, added a bit of red, and attached the rectangles to a background.

Are the rectangles all exactly the same size or angle? Are the strips all the same width? Are the pieces all straight? Of course not. But that's okay because in a free-form, no-pattern, modern world, nothing needs to be perfect.

Floating Rectangles by Rayna Gillman, 13″ × 19″, 2015

WHAT ELSE CAN YOU DO WITH RECTANGLES?

Until now we have kept things simple and minimalist. But if you have extra 3″ × 6″ units and some smaller pieces left, you can slice, dice, and put them together into an improv block. If you add white all around, you can probably picture a modern quilt like this, with no two blocks exactly alike but all related.

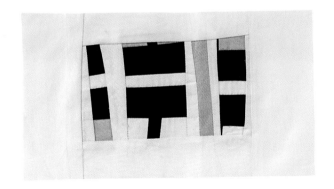

Are you ready to play? Try these ideas:

- Add one more color to your black, white, and medium color.

- Don't be afraid to cut up the rectangles without a plan. You'll be amazed at what you can make once you start slicing, rearranging, and adding strips, squares, and other pieces.

- Leave irregular edges on the units and place them on a background. Your finished piece will probably be a regular shape, but what's inside that shape doesn't have to be.

- Audition backgrounds—maybe something other than white or gray will look fabulous.

- Nancy added hot pink bits to her improvised black, white, and olive quilt (below) and put it on a black background. It is effective and dramatic.

Flamingo Jazz by Nancy B. Blake, 17¾˝ × 21½˝, 2016

Try playing with rectangles in a variety of sizes, colors, and values and see what the possibilities are. I'm sure you can come up with even more ideas for these simple shapes. There's no end to what you can do with fat, skinny, and classic rectangles! Whether you fuse or piece them, you can create your own free-form modern rectangle series.

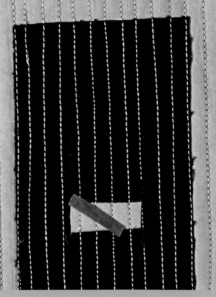

A WORD ABOUT FUSING

Most modern quilts seem to be pieced, but like rotary cutters and die-cutting machines, fusibles are tools that can make your life easier. If you prefer to fuse there is no reason not to. Sometimes it's the best way to go. This is especially true if you choose to leave irregular edges, as Nancy Blake did in *Flamingo Jazz* (previous page). You can sew the units together, add ½˝ of fusible web around the edges, and fuse it down. This eliminates the need to do a lot of irregular piecing of the background fabric and is one more way to add flexibility to your free-form approach to modern quiltmaking.

THE ART OF IMPROVISING

A JOURNEY WITHOUT A MAP

If you enjoy going for a drive without knowing where you'll end up, you may like to improvise when you are making quilts. However, if your GPS is always on and you need to know where you are going and how to get there before you leave home, you may find working without a pattern to be a challenge.

Improvising is saying or doing something on the spur of the moment, changing direction as you go along. Jazz musicians improvise, as do visual artists. And actors improvise (especially if they can't remember their lines). Does it always work? No. But it doesn't matter because they can switch gears—and often do. So can you!

Improvisational piecing lets you make decisions as you go along, without overthinking. Scrap quilts tend to be improvisational—that's what gives them individuality. But improvised piecing doesn't automatically yield good design.

GOOD DESIGN IS SLOW DESIGN

Slow design is the process of designing a piece on the wall, taking time to let it rest, checking that the design works as a composition, and rearranging the elements as needed.

Perhaps you have made a Log Cabin quilt with a bag of light strips and a bag of dark strips, picking blind and using whatever you grabbed. Despite the lack of advance planning, your quilt looked great because you took the time to arrange and rearrange the blocks into a harmonious whole that pleased your eye. That is slow design.

A TALE OF WOE AND A UFO

Here's what happened some time ago when I didn't use slow design. While cleaning my studio, I found a pile of leftover rectangles that all had a center stripe. I needed a baby quilt, so I cut them into small pieces and added strips of different colors and sizes, knowing that the common element would help unite them.

The blocks turned out well, but there still weren't enough. I was lazy, so instead of making more, I added a pile of random leftover blocks, thinking the quilt would have an improv, scrappy look. When I had pieced it together, I didn't like it but I thought adding borders would improve it. I should have known better.

Design? What design?

Photo by Rayna Gillman

It went from bad to worse. The result was disorganized, cluttered, and lacking in design. I sighed, put the top into the UFO pile, and went shopping for a baby gift.

what went wrong?

I had put the top together helter-skelter, with no thought to design, so it lacked the basic design elements that would have made it a cohesive piece. Consider the following design principles.

focal point

While not everything needs a focal point, there should be a place for the eye to start and end as it works its way around the piece. There was no visual path and nowhere to rest the eye.

balance

There was none. Everything was crowded together. In addition, multiple borders, unrelated to the center, added to the confusion.

unity and harmony

There needed to be a relationship between the pieces—either design, color, shape, or line. All those unrelated pieces created dissonance.

repetition and rhythm

The original blocks with a common element were lost in the crowd of random blocks. The result was chaos.

variety

There was too much variety and not enough common ground. Too many lines were going in different directions.

FROM NO DESIGN TO GOOD DESIGN

Recently, I took the quilt top apart. The original units went into a pile, and I threw the add-ons into the trash.

I auditioned several design options as I looked for a new layout. The first two worked, but they weren't "it," so I kept going until I was happy. Let's look at the choices to see what worked and why.

---

option 1

I could have stopped here because there was a sense of movement, as the blocks danced and seemed to talk to one another. My eye zigzagged back and forth from top to bottom, across the rows. The composition worked, but I didn't want a nine-patch.

option 2

This worked well because the center block pulled my eye in, up, and around the quilt, as the rectangles floated in a circle. But I wasn't sure.

Photo by Rayna Gillman

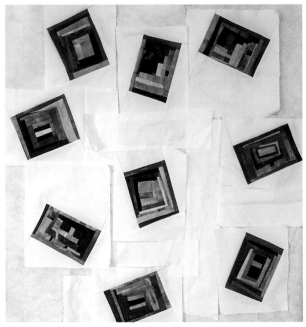

Photo by Rayna Gillman

third time was a charm

Once I clustered the blocks together into a medallion, I knew this was "it." The composition just felt right.

See-Saw by Rayna Gillman, 33″ × 34½″, 2016

Detail of *See-Saw* (at left)— repeated colors, repeated shapes

why does the medallion design work?

Focal point   The center medallion is the focal point, and the eye is likely to travel from left to right around the piece. Negative space gives the eye a place to rest and lets the center medallion breathe.

Balance   The left and right sides of the medallion have equal weight even though they are not exactly symmetrical.

Unity and harmony   The colors are varied but the pink and blue are distributed throughout, creating a dialogue and leading the eye.

Repetition and rhythm   The shapes and the colors repeat, and each unit has a kernel of a rectangle-with-strip somewhere in the block.

Variety   While the rectangles are similar, they are all slightly different in shape and content.

See-Saw succeeds because the parts relate to each other instead of being thrown together randomly, as they were in the original baby quilt.

Improvisation works best when it is combined with thoughtfulness as you begin to put the pieces together into a whole composition. That's the slow design process.

LEARNING TO SEE

Looking and seeing are two different things. When you are in the throes of working on a piece, you are often so involved with looking at it that you can't really *see* it. When you start getting tired or unsure, walk away for a while. Leave the work on your wall, and come back an hour or two later, or even the next day.

If you are by yourself, this is where your camera or smartphone comes in. If you are with another person, sometimes that is even better.

---

see through the camera's eye

Your smartphone or camera is your best friend and an indispensable tool. Take photos as you work, and look at them on the screen or on your computer. Because the images are relatively small, you can view your work as if from a distance, and you will see things you can't see when you are on top of the piece. If there are flaws, the camera will see them—and so will you.

see through someone else's eyes

A fresh pair of eyes can see your work in a new way, so it can be useful to let another artist whose work and opinion you respect take a look. This person does not have to be a quilter; he or she can be a painter, a printmaker, a photographer—the medium doesn't matter.

If you don't already belong to a small critique group, find a friend. Get together periodically to look at each other's works in progress and use the questions on the next pages as guidelines to help you see what works and what doesn't. Ask each other questions beginning with "What if … ?" or "What if you … ?" and then try each other's suggestions. Sometimes they will lead to an improvement, sometimes not. But looking at someone else's work with a critical (*not criticizing*) eye will help you see your own more clearly. This is especially important when you work improvisationally.

HOW TO EVALUATE A DESIGN

Chances are, you work alone most of the time. When you come to a stopping point, step back, take a look at your piece in progress, and ask yourself the questions that follow. They will help you determine whether the composition is working and why or why not. And by the way, if something is bothering you when you look at your piece, there is probably a good reason for it. These questions should help you discover what it is.

design questions

Where does my eye go first?

If it lands smack in the middle, is that where you want it to go? If yes, what makes your eye move elsewhere? If no, move the offending element off-center and see what else needs to be fixed.

Do the various elements talk to each other?

Do the colors repeat? Do the shapes repeat? Are fabric prints, like circles or lines, repeated elsewhere in the piece?

TIP: Repetition does not have to be exact. If you're using red, you don't need to use the identical shade or amount of red every time you repeat it. If your fabrics have stripes, they can be thin or thick, close together or wide apart. Circles can be spirals and dots, large and small.

Have I varied the scale?

If you are using prints and they are all the same size, your quilt may be less interesting than if you were to use small, medium, and large prints.

Is there enough contrast?

Sometimes you have a good reason for using similar values in a piece. But even if you deliberately make a low-contrast piece, there should still be a range of values. You may use primarily medium tones, but if you add even a few small touches of light and dark your piece will come alive. Look at it using the black-and-white setting on your smartphone, your tablet, or your computer. You will know immediately if the piece is all the same value.

Is there a line that goes off the edge and takes my eye out of the quilt?

Perhaps you need to move it elsewhere. This is especially risky when you use diagonals.

TIP: Diagonals give energy to a piece, but they need to stay away from the edges or they will take your viewer's eye right out of the work. Diagonals are challenging to use effectively; too few and that's where your attention goes. You need enough to make them an integral part of the design. How many is enough? Your eye will tell you.

Is the design balanced?

A design doesn't have to be symmetrical to be balanced; it can be asymmetrical and still be balanced. You will know whether it is top-heavy or bottom-heavy. Is there too much dark in one part of the quilt and too much light in another part? Is there something that anchors the piece at the bottom? Is there a shape in one spot that is out of proportion to everything else? Learn to trust your eye.

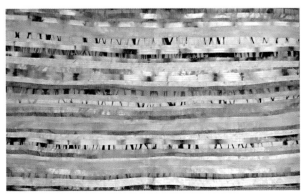

This is a low-contrast piece in neutrals, but there are tiny bits of black that keep it from being bland.

Photo by Rayna Gillman

Which orientation is best for this quilt?

At some point, rotate your quilt in all four directions. Often, a composition will work better in one direction than in the others. You will be amazed at how different it looks in each orientation.

Before your piece is put together, you can do this with your camera. Take a photo and rotate it; sometimes you can see a design flaw and correct it.

Even when everything looks good and you have finished the top, rotate it in all four directions. If someone else can lend his or her opinion, so much the better. Sometimes a horizontal piece wants to be a vertical, or vice versa. This quilt is a perfect example. I made it as a horizontal, but when I turned it vertically it became a stand of birch trees!

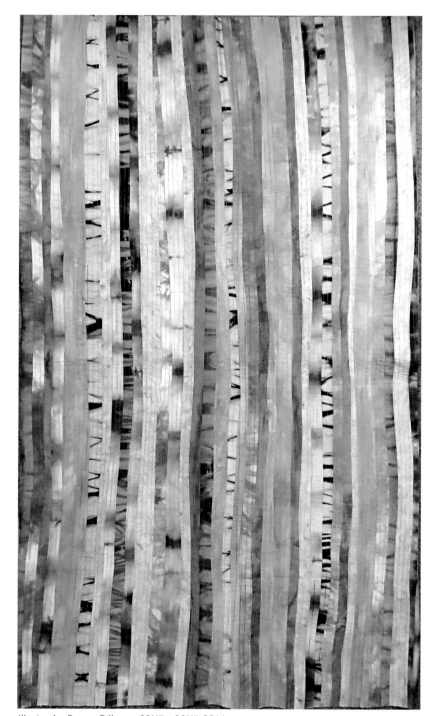

Illusion by Rayna Gillman, 23½˝ × 39½˝, 2014

Photo by Rayna Gillman

MODERN IMPROV WITH STRIPS

Unless you are brand new to quiltmaking, you probably have a bag of leftover strips and trimmings from previous projects. If you are new, you may not have accumulated too many of these skinny rectangles. In that case, of course, you will want to cut some (as if you need an excuse to cut fabric).

PICK UP YOUR RULER AGAIN

If you have yardage or fat quarters you haven't used yet, this is a good time to slice 2½˝ strips across the widths. If you are using precut strips such as jelly roll strips, which are 44˝ long, fold them into quarters and cut each into 4 pieces, each 11˝ long. Or, cut off a manageable length anywhere between 8˝ and 12˝. You don't need to be exact; you just need a length that is comfortable to slice and sew.

NOW, PUT DOWN YOUR RULER

Now that you've measured, you can slice the strips freehand. Cutting without a ruler will give your strips a soft, organic edge; emphasize the improvisational look of your quilt; and liberate you from "precision angst" so you can relax and work stress-free.

The more relaxed you are, the more fun you will have. The more fun you have, the more spontaneous and original your quilts will be. How can you go wrong?

When you start with 2½˝-wide strips, it's easy to slice them into thinner strips of varying widths.

1. Cut a strip in half lengthwise. Estimate by eye and slice. Don't try to make the cut curvy; when you try to cut straight without a ruler, a gentle curve will develop on its own.

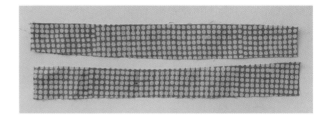

2. Cut another strip approximately in thirds, estimating by eye.

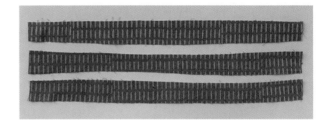

When you sew the strips together, you will be able to see the gentle curves.

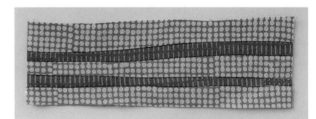

If you plan to work in all solids, cut a variety of colors and values, varying the widths as on page 37.

If you want more options, cut enough prints so you will have lots of choices and can combine them with each other and/or with solids as the mood strikes.

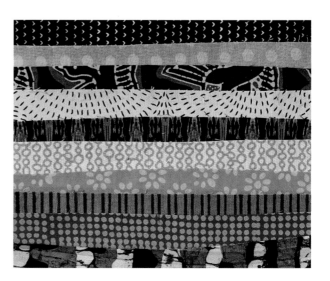

MAKE STRIPS PART OF YOUR INVENTORY

After you have cut a variety of colors, values, prints, and sizes, throw the strips into a plastic box, bag, or basket and you'll have a strip stash ready when you start improvising for your next piece. All you need to do is select the ones you want to use and sew them together.

If you don't have large blocks of time, sew some strips together when you have a few minutes. Or, add leftover strips from trimmings when you have finished a piece. Widths can vary—anything from ½˝ and up works. If the strips are as wide as a few inches, just trim them down when you are ready to use them.

Rachel Cochran reached into her pile of leftover strips and made an improvised nine-patch. The white background gives it a clean, fresh look.

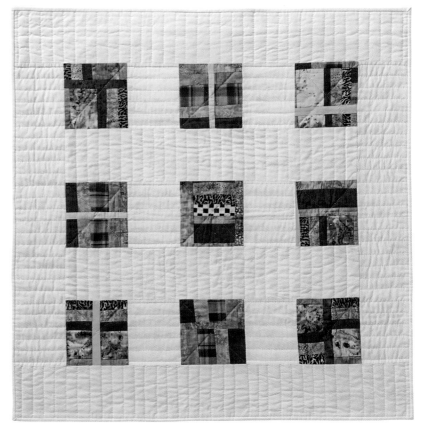

Scrappy Nine by Rachel B. Cochran, 35˝ × 35˝, 2015

Diane Fama pieced her strips improvisationally using a limited palette. She had an idea of what she wanted but didn't overplan. Instead, she designed and modified as she went along. After she had sewn the strips together, she cut them into wedges and arranged them until she was happy with the result. The combination of improv piecing and slow design resulted in a circular modern medallion.

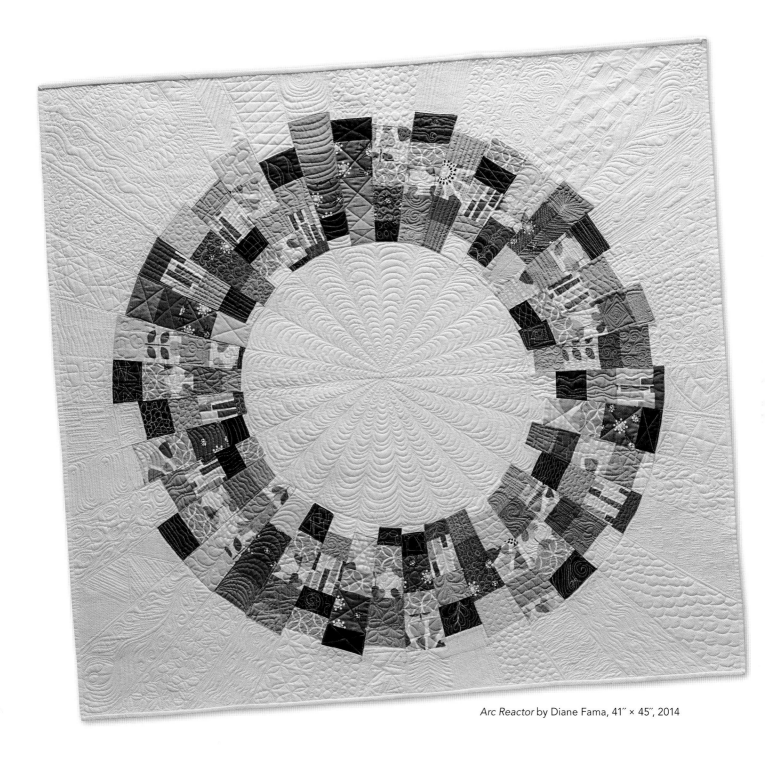

Arc Reactor by Diane Fama, 41″ × 45″, 2014

MODERN STRING QUARTET

UPDATING AN OLD FAVORITE

If you ever want to make a real no-brainer, fool-proof quilt with your strips, you can always make a string quilt. String quilts are among the oldest and simplest quilts to make. My first blocks (long lost) were string blocks a friend of my mother's taught me to make, a decade before I took my first quilt class in 1974.

Today, string quilts are back (if they ever went away), and they lend themselves perfectly to the modern aesthetic. Wonky lines, improvisational designs, secondary patterns, negative space—all of these can be achieved with strings (freehand-cut strips). With a "what if?" approach, I experimented with the classic string quilt and found a way to make an old-fashioned string quilt in a new-fashioned way.

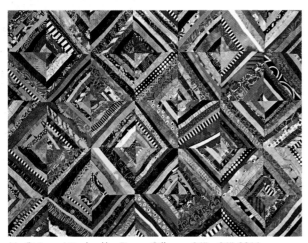

No Strings Attached by Rayna Gillman, 36″ × 24″, 2014
Photo by Rayna Gillman

You probably know that the traditional way to make a string quilt is by sewing all the strips to a paper foundation and tearing off the paper between stitching lines when you are done. This tedious, time-consuming method was no doubt the original way to make a paper-pieced quilt. I used this method for years, until the light went on in my head.

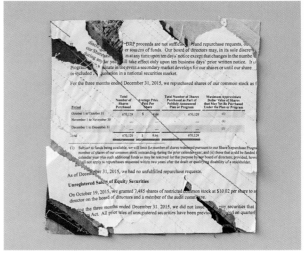

Photo by Rayna Gillman

Here's my gift to you: the secret to making a string quilt with only one line of stitching through the paper.

Relax! Seams don't have to be ¼″ and points don't have to match. Pick up your leftover strips, or the ones you recently cut, and get busy. This will be fun!

Strings in Half-Time
by Rayna Gillman, machine quilted
by Diane Fama (see full quilt, page 46)

STRING QUARTET 1: NO STRINGS ATTACHED

1. Start as usual by placing a strip diagonally across a square of paper. I am making these 6˝ × 6˝ squares, but they can be any size you like.

2. Place the next string on top of the first and sew through the paper. This will be the only line of stitching through the paper backing.

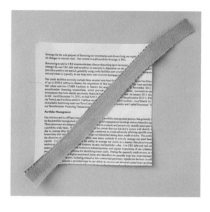

If the strips slip a little off-center as you sew, don't worry; the quilt will just be more interesting. Keep going!

3. Open the strip and fold the paper back out of the way in the opposite direction from the side where you are adding.

Open the strips.

Fold back the paper.

4. With both halves of the paper to one side, sew on the next strip.

Sew strips to each other with the paper out of the way.

TIP: When you add strips to the other side of the center strip, fold the paper in the opposite direction.

5. These strips have been sewn to each other, not to the paper. Only the first 2 strips are sewn to the paper.

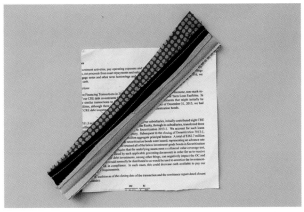
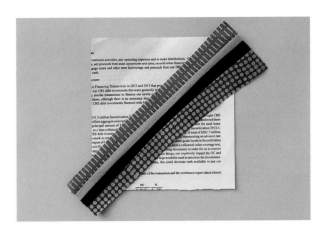

The undersides of the strips are sewn to each other.

---

6. When you have sewn a number of strips to each side, open the paper and press the strips flat to see how many more you need to add. You can keep going, using slightly shorter strips, or you may decide to cover the rest of the triangle with one piece of fabric as you get a bit closer to the tip.

Depending on the width and number of strings used, all the blocks will be different.

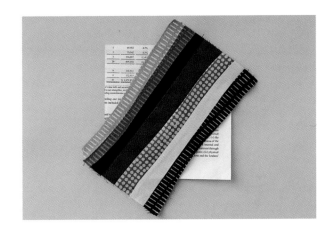

TIP: A quick press with the iron every so often will keep the strips flat as you add to them. You can also use shorter strips as you get closer to the edge.

7. After the paper is covered, turn it over and use your ruler and the paper as a guide to trim the piece into a square.

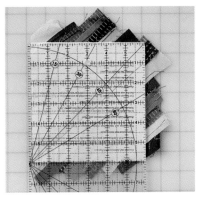

8. Tear off the paper. It will take a nanosecond, since there is only one line of stitching.

Back of the block. One line of stitching is all you need.

These four blocks are made with only one line of stitching through each paper square. No stress, no mess, no frustration! Solids and contemporary batiks give a modern look to a classic block.

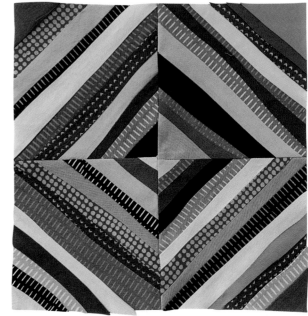

Front of the block

STRING QUARTET 2: PLAYING IN HALF-TIME

If you are feeling lazy, you can make a beautiful modern string quilt with half the work and no need for paper. Half the square is a solid triangle and the other half is made of strips. You will make 2 blocks from every square you cut.

1. Cut squares from solid fabric, whatever size and color you like. These are 6″ × 6″ squares.

2. Slice them in half at a 45° angle so you have 2 equal triangles from each square.

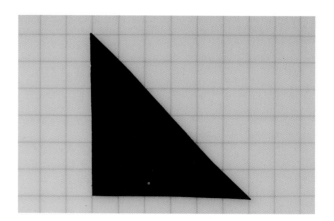

3. Sew the first strip to the diagonal edge and add a few more strips. You will be trimming as you go along, so turn the square over and iron the points of the triangle toward the strips. This will ensure that they don't get chopped off when you trim.

Press the triangle tips toward the strips.

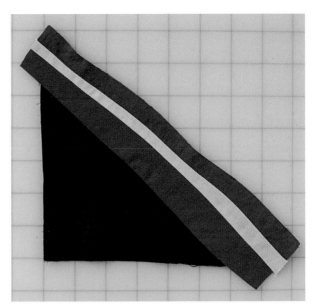

Strips added to the triangle

- -

4. Trim for the size of block you are making.

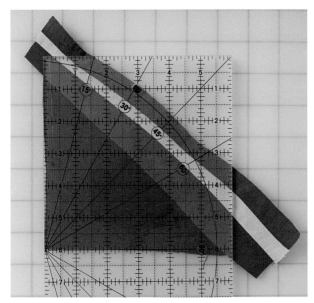

Trim along the sides of the ruler.

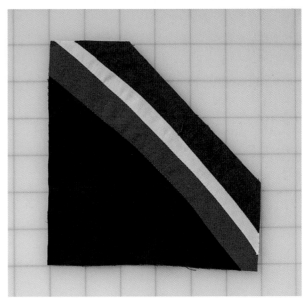

Trim as you go.

Now you see that you can add shorter strips as you move closer to the tip of the triangle. If you have leftover strips or trimmings from another block, you can use the shorter ones.

These half-square triangle strings can be set many different ways and used with a variety of color palettes, sizes, and any combination of solids and/or prints.

Add shorter strips as you approach the tip.

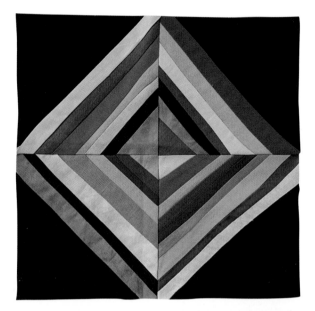

The solids and dark fabric are a nod to Amish quilts from centuries ago—yet the alternate grid brings the quilt into the modern age.

Can you imagine this quilt in a limited color palette, a lighter background with blocks of varied scales, or set differently? Try your own variation.

Strings in Half-Time
by Rayna Gillman,
machine quilted
by Diane Fama,
72″ × 90″, 2016

STRING QUARTET 3: A LITTLE OFF-KEY

My "what if?" kicked in again, as I wondered what would happen if I didn't use a ruler and didn't cut the square in half but just cut off a corner at a random angle.

The angles on these blocks are all different because I cut them freehand. The result is a whimsical quilt with an irregular secondary motif, depending on how you quilt the space.

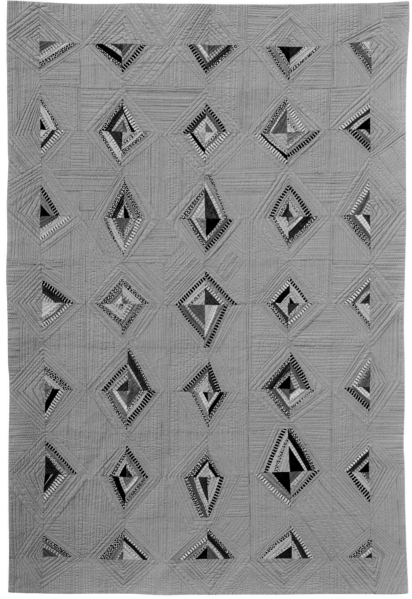

Go Fly a Kite by Rayna Gillman, quilted by Diane Fama, 36″ × 52″, 2016

This quilt was especially fun to make (and is still fun to look at) because of the varied sizes and shapes!

how to make your own version

1. Cut a bunch of squares. (Yes, "a bunch" is a legitimate number if you are experimenting.) You can make them any size you like. If you're making a bed quilt, you might want to cut them 6½″ × 6½″, which gives you 12″ × 12″ finished blocks. My version uses 4½″ × 4½″ squares, which finish to 8″ × 8″.

2. Stack 4 squares together and slice off a corner at any angle: large and sharp, small and gentle, or anything in between. Do not use a ruler and don't overthink. Just cut and you can't go wrong.

3. When you're tired of slicing off corners and have enough to work with, separate the squares from the cut-off corners, put them into a pile, pick one at random, and add free-cut strips to the diagonal edge. When you have added several strips, use your ruler and trim the piece to the desired size (in this case a 4½″ × 4½″ square, which gives a finished block of 8″ × 8″).

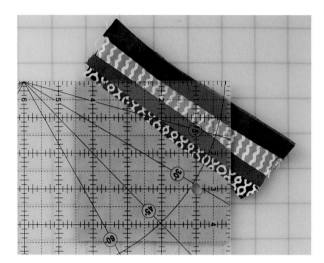

4. Repeat until you have 16 squares, which are enough to give you a start. Arrange 4 pieces until they suit your eye.

TIP: If there is still a bit of empty space at the tip of the corner, use a trimming or small scrap, as you only need a bit of fabric.

WORKING THE ANGLE

When you cut without measuring, you will end up with pieces in a variety of sizes and shapes. In the following examples, you will notice that the top end of the left square is much narrower than its bottom left side. In the right-hand square there is only a slight difference between the two edges.

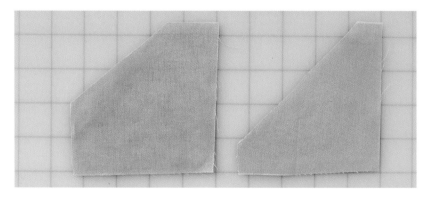

Because the angles vary, the blocks will look different depending on how you arrange them.

It's fun to play with the possibilities; you can make some blocks more regular than others if you choose to. Here are two different arrangements of the same pieces.

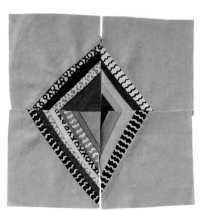

More regular

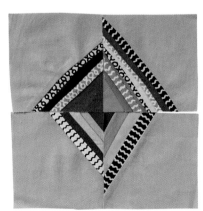

More playful

CREATE YOUR OWN IMPROV QUILTS

For a true improv quilt, don't worry about whether the angles match each other when you put them together. In fact, don't even try to match them; let the pieces fall where they may. It's more fun that way and there is an element of surprise, which is what the free-form, improvise-as-you-go approach is all about.

I sewed together these two blocks as I picked up each piece. Even without planning, one is more evenly matched than the other. Regardless, no two blocks will be identical and all of them will look terrific when they are sewn together—so don't obsess over how they go together.

TIP: One of the tricks to making a successful free-form modern scrap quilt is to repeat the colors and fabrics often enough to create unity.

OTHER DESIGN OPTIONS

The benefit of working pattern-free is that you can vary the size, the scale, the colors, and the fabrics according to your mood. This block's yellow background, polka dots, and high-contrast fabrics would make a lively modern improv quilt for a baby or toddler.

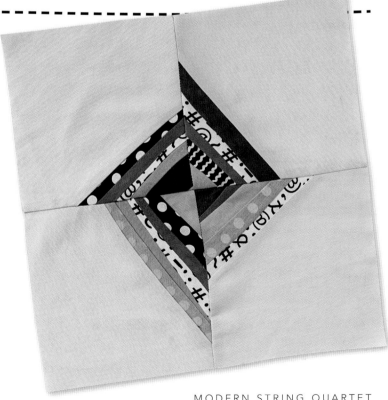

using a limited palette

This example uses only solids in neutrals plus one bright color, which you can vary from block to block. If you arrange the angles to create a more uniform look and make the center the same as the background, the focus will be on the diamond shape. This will give a super-modern, sophisticated feel to the quilt!

- -

using a patterned background

Yes, a patterned background! These blocks are on Laura Lechner's design wall. I must admit the thought never occurred to me, but this student's "what-if?" led her to use a patterned fabric for her squares. The irregular dots work beautifully with the strings, and when the quilt is finished it will be a knockout!

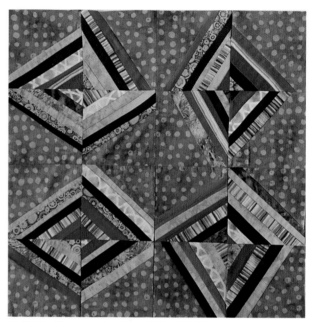

Unfinished by Laura Lechner, 22″ × 22″, 2016

Photo by Daniel A. Ginsburg

- -

STRING QUARTET 4: VARIATIONS ON A THEME

What if, instead of cutting off the corner, you started your no-ruler slice 1″ or so in from the edge and cut a wedge instead of a triangle? I tried it and discovered a wealth of modern variations.

I cut these without a ruler, eyeballing the angle to avoid uniformity. But you can easily use a ruler if you want the angles to be exactly the same. You may also want to experiment with cutting a wider angle, starting ½″ in from the corner and ending at about 3″.

1 *Cut 16 squares.*

The minimum number of squares you need to try out a variety of arrangements is 8; 16 squares is even better because you will have more design options.

I used 6″ × 6″ squares, but any size will work. If you are making a bed-size quilt, you may want to cut the squares larger to give you more negative space. If you are working on a mini for the wall, you can cut the squares smaller to keep the blocks in proportion to the size of the quilt.

2 *Slice a wedge from each square.*

Place a square (or squares if you want to cut 4 at once) on the cutting mat. Using the lines as guides, start about 1″ in from the edge of the square and cut across to approximately the 2″ mark on the opposite side. When you cut, eyeball the angle to avoid uniformity; the cuts will be similar but not exactly the same. If you want a more uniform look, you may want to use a ruler.

Remove the wedge you have sliced off. You will add strips to replace the wedge you have removed. Do this for all the squares.

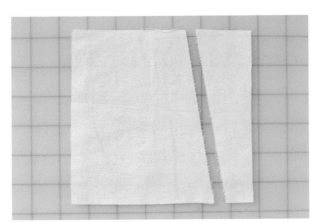

Start the cut at about the 1″ mark and end at about the 2″ mark.

TIP: The cut-off wedges will give you a good start on another piece at some point. Throw them into your box of leftovers.

3 *When you have 8 or 16 squares, put half of them in a pile with the cut angle away from you and the top of the slope on the right.*

Let's call this the A block.

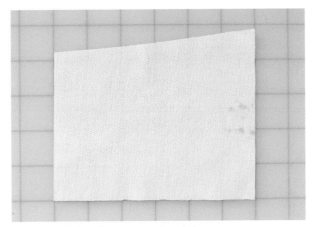

The top of the slope is on the right.

4 *Put the other half of the squares in a pile with the cut sloping down from the left.*

You now have two piles of sliced squares facing in opposite directions, and you're going to add strips to all of them, keeping them facing in opposite directions.

This is the B block.

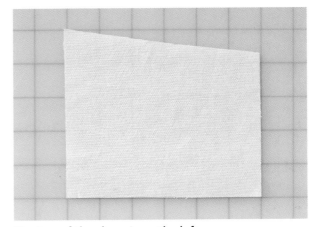

The top of the slope is on the left.

5 *Using the fabrics of your choice, sew 4 or 5 strips to the angled edge.*

Use your ruler to measure as you add, and when you have enough strips, trim to a 6″ × 6″ square. Do this with all the blocks.

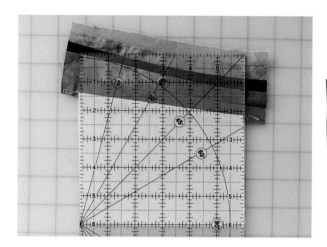

> **TIP:** Be sure to cut the strips long enough to leave at least ½″ on either side of the square. Because you are sewing at an angle, looks can be deceptive—you may have enough height on one end but not on the other. Don't trim until you have enough height to measure a 6″ × 6″ square.

imagine the possibilities

After you have trimmed the blocks, you'll discover how versatile they are. The A blocks and B blocks are opposites, and that's what makes them fun to play with. Ask yourself "what if?" and try different arrangements.

Alternate grid 1: Three-dimensional   If you put the A and B blocks with the wide parts together, they look somewhat three-dimensional. What if the white fabric in the blocks on the left were slightly darker? Would the 3D be even more pronounced? It's a what-if for another time.

Alternate grid 2: Whimsical   These have a whimsical feel, as the blocks dance in different directions.

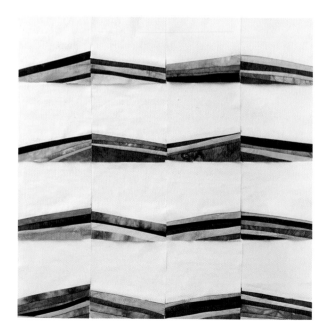

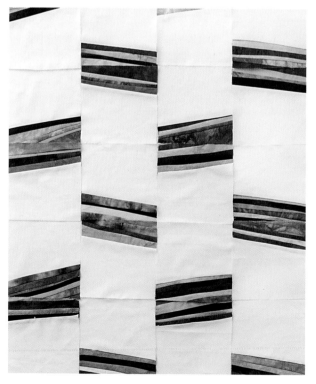

Alternate grid 3: Structured A more structured look as they fly in formation. The block repeats in the same direction.

Alternate grid 4: Lanterns Placed end to end for a more linear look.

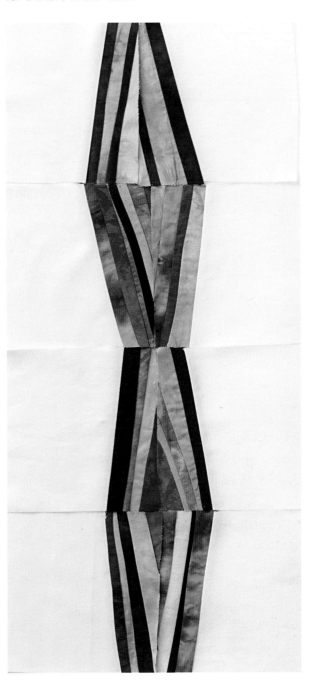

Alternate grid 5: Star Placing the large ends together creates a different look.

Alternate grid 6: Windmill The small ends are placed together at the center.

If you put four Windmill blocks together, a secondary pattern will emerge from the negative space. Because the angles are irregular, the negative spaces will be slightly varied as well.

I hope you'll be inspired to use these what-ifs to try your own variations. Here are a few more ideas for you.

Tilting at Windmills by Rayna Gillman, 20¾˝ × 20¾˝, 2016

MORE IDEAS

What if you used one fabric for the wedge instead of strips?

What if you used prints for the wedges instead of solids?

What if you used patterned fabrics for both parts of the block? You could set these in an alternate grid, perhaps on point, with a white background.

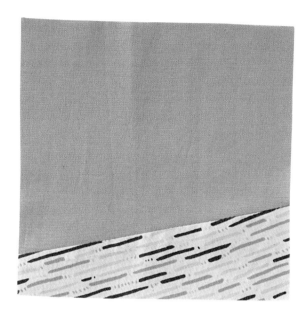

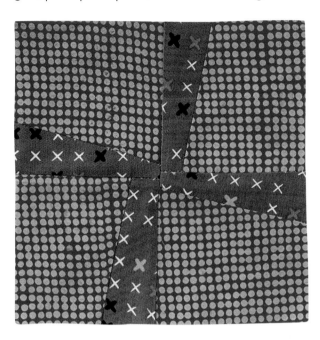

TIP: Cut 2 squares the same size and slice them together. You will have 2 of each piece. Save the alternate pieces to use later in a modern scrap quilt.

Sew together and save for later.

TIP: When you are using prints, most of which are not reversible, pay attention when you cut the A and B background blocks because you can't turn them over as you can with solids.

Have fun with strings in all their variations—even if the variation is a very wide string that looks like a wedge!

IMPROV PAPER PIECING

This may sound like an oxymoron, because when we think of paper piecing we think of precision. Historically, paper foundations with pattern lines printed on them and numbered in sequence were made for complex traditional patterns that might require perfect piecing. Today, there are books and patterns for modern quilters who want to try this method for accuracy.

I paper pieced a block eons ago for an invitational exhibit. Each artist had to make a traditional block and interpret its name in a nontraditional way. I chose the Palm block, and because the pieces were small I thought I would try paper piecing. But I am not a perfectionist, and the process was so stressful for me that I swore never to do it again. And I haven't—until now.

Palm Tree by Rayna Gillman, 18″ × 18″, 1999
Photo by Rayna Gillman

A PROBLEM AND A SOLUTION

When I made *Strings in Half-Time* (page 46) I had a pile of trimmings and offcuts, mostly small triangles that I hated to throw away. I sewed some of them together into whimsical houses and put them aside while I used the other triangles for a mini quilt.

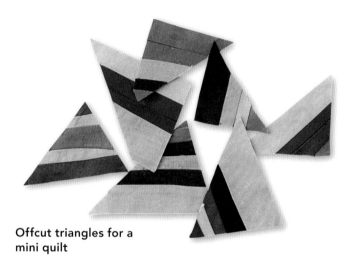

Offcut triangles for a mini quilt

Problem The triangles' sizes and shapes varied, but I wanted all the blocks to be the same size.

What-if While my decades-ago flirtation with paper piecing had ended badly, I wondered if a paper foundation would make it easier to work with the random-sized triangles. What if I were to revisit the process, ruler-free and without printed lines, a numerical sequence, or precision? If I worked with already-pieced centers, as these triangles were, there would be less paper to tear off!

Solution A template-free foundation

NO-PATTERN PAPER PIECING

Paper piecing can be a good way to use up those leftover offcuts, odd-shaped bits, or cut-up blocks that didn't fit into that last quilt (or the one before that). Improvised paper-pieced quilts don't require the precision of traditional blocks, so you don't need lines or numbers on your paper. Simply cut a paper foundation into a square or rectangle of any size or shape and get started.

This is a very adaptable way to work. You can start with one scrap of fabric or an already-pieced center, make it large-scale, add a solid background to each block, use an alternate grid layout, or make it totally scrappy.

here's how it works

The paper for these blocks is 3½″ × 6″, but this method works for any shape and size of foundation.

1. Place the center piece on the paper.

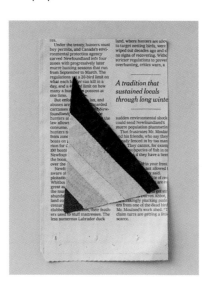

2. Cut a piece of background fabric wide enough and long enough to cover the blank space and overlap the paper slightly. Sew it facedown to one edge of the triangle and flip.

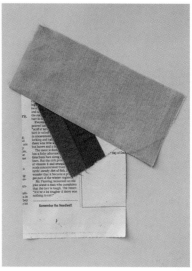

Sew and flip.

- -

3. Press and trim the fabric to the size of the paper.

4. Keep adding fabric until the paper is covered, trimming as you go.

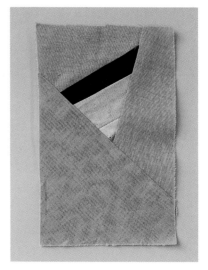

minimal tearing away

Because only three pieces of fabric were sewn to the paper, there was hardly anything to tear away. This was a treat! "Now," I thought, "how else can I use this technique?" It was time to experiment again and find some other options.

what paper is best?

Any thin paper works well, from old phone book pages to newsprint. Some people use copy paper, but copy paper is heavy to sew through and difficult to tear away, and will dull your needle quickly. Since my newspapers are delivered daily, I have plenty of recyclable foundation material.

Copy paper is difficult to remove.

(No, the ink does not transfer to the fabric.) If you read your news online, you can buy a pad of newsprint or use a foundation paper such as Carol Doak's Foundation Paper (by C&T Publishing).

- -

OTHER IMPROV PAPER-PIECED IDEAS

not-quite square-in-a-square

This is an improvised riff on the traditional Square-in-a-Square block, which means that no two blocks will be the same.

TIP: When you are improvising blocks that will all be different, a limited palette, repeated colors, or repeated fabrics will help create unity.

method 1: paper piece the entire block

1. Place the free-cut fabric on a square of paper. Center squares don't have to be a uniform size or exactly square. Finished sizes will also vary from block to block, which is part of their charm.

2. Using the sew-and-flip method, add improvisationally around the center until you are happy with the size.

3. Trim stray threads and add the corner pieces.

Adding the rest of the corner pieces will add a few more stitching lines, but this simple block will not have many pieces of paper to remove.

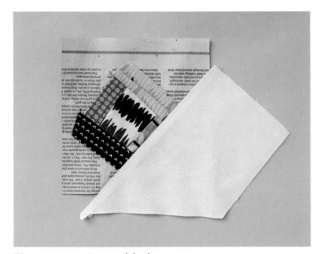

First corner piece added

Back of paper

4. Trim the block to size and remove the paper.

The larger or more complex the center motif, the more paper pieces you will have to tear off.

My solution?

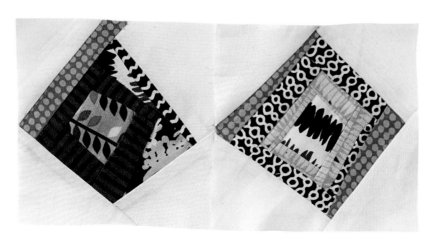

method 2: paper piece just the corners

1. Improvise your blocks first; then place them on the paper.

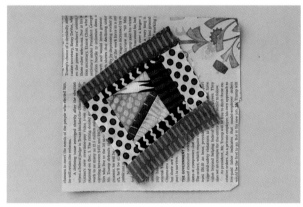

Not attached to paper yet

2. Add the corner pieces, stitching through the paper; then trim to size and remove the paper. Using the paper—even if just for the corners—stabilizes the bias edges or the corners, making it easier to trim. And, best of all, you know the exact size you are aiming for.

Because you have pieced most of the block before placing it on the paper, you will have only four lines of stitching through the paper—one for each diagonal corner!

modern crazy quilt blocks

This may sound like an oxymoron because the words *modern* and *crazy quilt* are not usually used in the same sentence. But they are not mutually exclusive. If you leave off the embellishments and fancy hand stitching and make a crazy quilt with the odd scraps you've collected, you'll have a modern aesthetic. This is especially true if you use all solids or surround your printed fabric with a solid.

option 1: piece directly on the paper

If you prefer to use a paper foundation for the entire block, by all means, go ahead. Set your stitch length to 1.5 so the paper will be easier to tear off.

This is a paper-pieced crazy block in process. As you can imagine, there were lots of stitching lines on the back and many small pieces of paper to remove.

In fact, there were so many layers of fabric and teeny paper bits to remove that I finally gave up. The back of the block reminded me why paper piecing drove me crazy (no pun intended) years ago.

Photo by Rayna Gillman

Back side of crazy block

But, of course, there is a fix for this!

option 2: keep the paper stitching to a minimum

1. Sew random scraps into units *before* you place them on the paper.

Before doing this …

Photo by Rayna Gillman

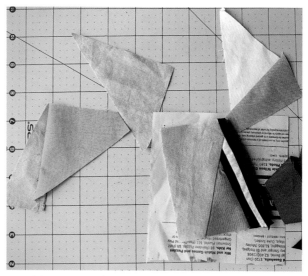

… add more random scraps.

Photo by Rayna Gillman

- -

2. Sew the pieced units to one another.

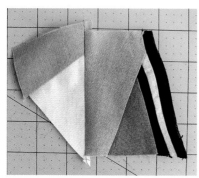

Photo by Rayna Gillman

3. Trim as needed.

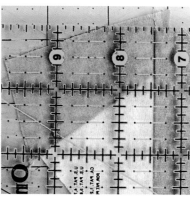

Photo by Rayna Gillman

Keep adding and trimming. Don't think too hard about the sizes or shapes of pieces. This is, after all, a crazy block.

4. When the unit is almost the size of the paper you've cut, place it where you'd like it on the foundation.

Photo by Rayna Gillman

5. Add enough fabric to cover the rest of the paper.

> **TIP:** You can add pieces without having to sew every one through the paper, as long as some are anchored. When a piece of fabric is anchored on only one side, you can add to the free side without putting an extra line of stitching through the paper. Do this whenever you can.

Modern crazy block

Green added to the free side of the black strip

Photo by Rayna Gillman

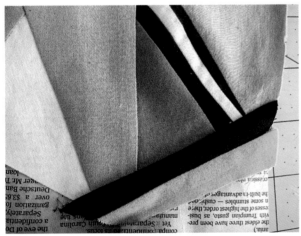

Photo by Rayna Gillman

The finished piece has only four lines of stitching through the paper because most of the sewing was done ahead of time.

As I found the workarounds to eliminate almost all the stitching lines, I could see the potential benefits of using a paper foundation for improvisational piecing. But it is not the only method for creating improvisational blocks.

In Improv Paper Piecing (page 56), you improvised without much paper when you pieced parts of the block *before* you placed them on the foundation (see Method 2: Paper Piece Just the Corners, page 60). Now you can omit the paper entirely because you will be using blocks that are already pieced together. Improv piecing from existing blocks can be easier than starting from scratch because you already have a jumping-off place.

A MODERN FEAST FROM LEFTOVERS

We all have them: experiments, leftovers (used or unused) from a quilt, or older blocks too traditional to fit into your new modern look. Why should they go to waste when you can stir the pot, add another ingredient or two, and make them even better? Your next modern quilt will thank you for it.

As always, when you work free-form, there is no one right way to remake your blocks. There are no rules or recipes. You can make them complex or keep them super simple.

The blocks just need to suit you and look good in a modern setting. So, get out some leftover blocks, your cutter, and cutting mat.

REMAKE UNUSED BLOCKS

This process began with a pile of leftover rectangles. The recreated blocks are not identical—since improvising means never getting the same result twice—but they will work together.

Leftover rectangles

don't be cautious

When you overthink before you cut, you risk losing your free working style—and it will show. That is exactly what happened here. Instead of just making a cut, I thought about what I would do with the two rectangles. I decided to cut one in half, slice a quarter from another, and sew them together. The result was graphic and I thought it had possibilities, so I made another. But because these were not improvised, they were almost identical. Planning ahead is the antithesis of improvisation—so it was time to stop thinking!

Almost identical

Remade but not improvised

It's only fabric, and if you work quickly and intuitively you'll be pleasantly surprised. I took the minimalist block and cut it, added other pieces, sewed, and cut again. This time, I didn't stop to think. And in the process, I created a block that is graphic, relatively simple, and unique. No danger of having the next one be a clone!

Added ingredients

New block

REVIVE BORING BLOCKS

What about those blocks that didn't turn out the way you had hoped? There's always something you can do. I made one block like this and thought it was dull. Time for triage!

Original block

Here are the steps I took, which you can follow when you look at the revived block.

1. Slice the block into 3 sections.

Photo by Rayna Gillman

2. Sew sections 1 and 3 together, forming the center of the new block.

3. Cut section 2 in half vertically (orange and gray strips).

4. Add pink to each side of the center and add the section 2 strips.

5. Add black-and-white squares (leftovers from something else).

Much better!

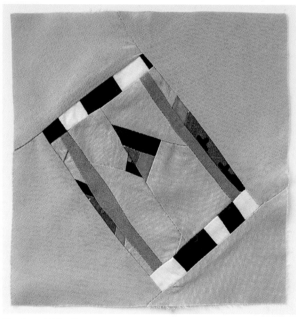

Revived block

REPURPOSE USED BLOCKS

Have you ever made a quilt, only to find that it didn't work or was just plain ugly? If the top is still sitting around in your closet, you have several choices. You can leave it there, taking up space; you can finish it as a charity quilt; or you can take it apart and improvise fresh, new blocks.

I am sorry to say that I recently had such an experience—the blocks didn't make up the way I wanted them to, but I went ahead and quilted the quilt anyway. Big mistake!

I not only *could* have quit, but *should* have. The triangles were not all the same width, and parts either overlapped or were cut off. That would have been okay if the triangles had been set differently, but the flaws were too obvious for what I was trying to achieve.

I took out enough of the quilting to salvage some of the blocks and began to repurpose them together with other blocks in other settings.

As with any improvisation, there are multiple ways to recreate or repurpose blocks, used or not. I hope the following gives you some ideas for your own repurposing adventures.

Original blocks

Photo by Rayna Gillman

My Instagram post

Photo by Rayna Gillman

TIP: You do not have to use every piece of your original blocks in the new blocks. If you have pieces left, put them aside or add them to something else.

Here are two possibilities for reworking those triangle blocks.

- *Cut a block or two vertically down the middle.* Insert a strip, add more triangles, or play with other ideas on your design wall. When you find an arrangement that you like, sew the pieces together.

- *Layer two blocks and cut them into horizontal sections.* Separate, alternate, rearrange, and sew some of the pieces together, adding other fabrics if you wish.

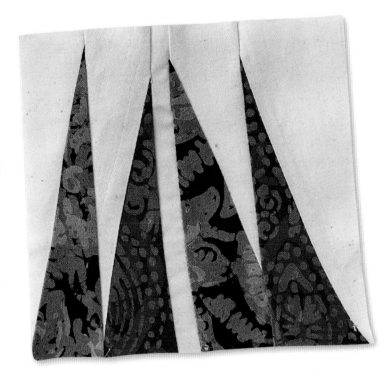

Photo by Rayna Gillman

Triangles cut horizontally

If the block is small, as this one is, you may want to add some other pieces to make it larger. In that case, the next step should not surprise you.

finish on a paper foundation

Both the original and the revived gray blocks (see Revive Boring Blocks, page 65) were made by laying the centers on paper squares and adding the corner triangles. The two blocks here, made in 2016, were crazy pieced without all the newspaper seams, as in Option 2: Keep the Paper Stitching to a Minimum (page 61).

In each case, you can see repurposed triangle blocks similar to those we have just worked with.

On the left are two that have been cut horizontally and rearranged; on the right are two triangle halves with a strip between them.

So, we've come full circle. We started and ended with improvisational paper piecing done the easy way, with a minimum number of stitching lines through the foundation. In between, we did some paperless piecing. Both methods are effective, and which one you use at any given time depends on what you are doing. In both cases, your blocks can have a modern look and can have a family resemblance without being exactly the same.

Triangles cut vertically

Photo by Rayna Gillman

When you are creating original work that doesn't follow a pattern, chances are you were inspired by something: a color, a line, a fabric, a feeling, a word, or an image. You may know where the inspiration came from or you may not realize it until the piece is finished.

I spoke to some of the artists whose improvisational work straddles the line between modern and art and asked them what informs their work and where their inspirations come from. Most of these pieces defy labeling; maybe labels aren't important. Or maybe we can label them "postmodern."

CATHERINE WHALL SMITH

Catherine explores the spaces created "where line meets line or lines overlap lines." She pairs her often-sinuous lines with the spaces between them to create movement and add vibrancy to her work. Improvisational cutting and piecing, negative space, solid fabrics, and a vivid palette make an art quilt with a modern edge.

Patterns, colors, and emerging lines are the themes of Catherine's quilts, which are inspired by the landscape in her rural surroundings. Line is the voice that narrates her stories of the cutting of the hay in the fields and the seasonal changes around her. She uses hand stitching as a way to connect with her work and to create the shapes and shadows of her environment.

Gold Hay #1 by Catherine Whall Smith, 27″ × 27″, 2011

CINDY GRISDELA

Cindy calls herself a contemporary art quilter, but what is not modern about these quilts? They are improvisationally pieced, minimalist and simple, and have negative space. Cindy is inspired by the work of abstract painters such as Matisse, Morris Louis, and Mark Rothko. Typically, she starts with either fabric that speaks to her or with a design idea, such as free-form circles or diagonal bands of color, and improvises from there.

Pearls by Cindy Grisdela, 19″ × 19″, 2014
Photo by Greg Staley

Cranberry Fields by Cindy Grisdela, 12″ × 12″, 2015
Photo by Greg Staley

Intuition by Cindy Grisdela, 30″ × 43″, 2010

Photo by Greg Staley

DEBBIE ANDERSON

Debbie is a quilt artist who follows her own path. Her architectural pieces emerged from the freedom to cut and piece without overthinking. These are part of a series that uses space, line, and color in unusual or unexpected ways. Debbie's houses are inspired by her childhood imagination. She invented these happy, colorful dwellings when she daydreamed of traveling from rural Alaska, where she grew up. She works intuitively, letting her fabric dictate the placement. As she cuts and sews, the places in her mind began to appear on her wall, seemingly by themselves.

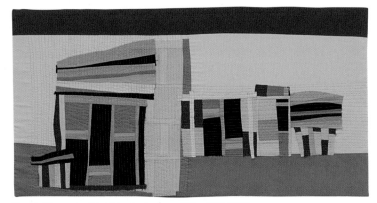

Beach House by Debbie Anderson, 42″ × 21″, 2016
Photo by Ellen Davis

Bamboo House by Debbie Anderson, 41″ × 29″, 2016
Photo by Ellen Davis

Fun House by Debbie Anderson, 40″ × 27″, 2016
Photo by Ellen Davis

PATTY ALTIER

Patty uses space, scale, and a limited palette to make this piece both modern and art. It is one of a series inspired by the stages in a professional bicycle race. The colors of the racers' jerseys, the twisty roads, the mountains, the aerial shots of the towns, the colors of the roofs from village to village, and the scenery are all influences. *Stage 10* is the tenth piece in the Stage series.

Stage 10
by Patty Altier,
31½″ × 50¼″, 2009

WHAT INSPIRES ME?

I have been working improvisationally for more than three decades, and my bodies of work have been variously influenced by the Holocaust; the urban landscape; memory and loss; and often a fabric, color, pattern, or image.

Sometimes I am inspired by an image but have to tuck it away for another time. At right are two textiles that inspire me with both color and pattern—put aside for the near future. I have already begun to play with fabrics in this palette and am motivated to get back to my design wall!

Below right is the piece that was on my design wall, created with rectangles and inspired by the palette in the African and Indian textiles above.

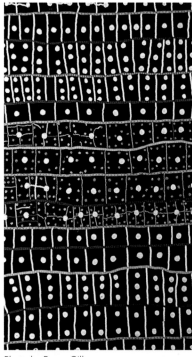

Photo by Rayna Gillman

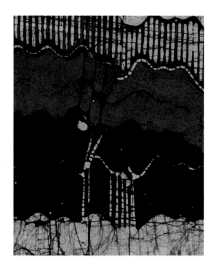

Design wall fabrics

Almost There
by Rayna Gillman,
24″ × 30″, 2017

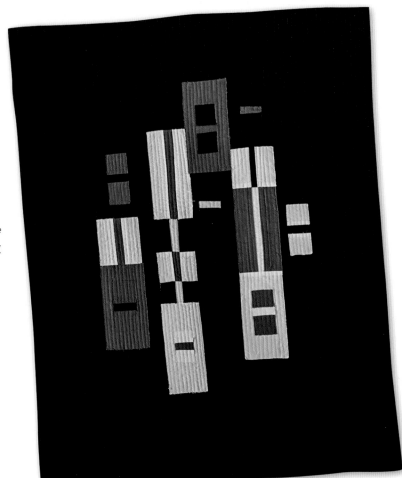

Most of the time I don't discover what has inspired me until a piece is done.

The quilt below was meant to be trees, inspired by the woods behind my house. But when it was finished, it was something else entirely—an echo of a photo I had taken and forgotten. My beloved New York skyline appeared out of my subconscious.

Storm Warning by Rayna Gillman, 37″ × 18½″, 2011
Photo by Rayna Gillman

Photo by Rayna Gillman

When you are working improvisationally and capturing the essence of an image, your quilt will probably not resemble the object that has inspired it. That was the case with this quilt (at right).

I named this quilt *deWaterkant* because the buildings in that neighborhood of Cape Town are a riot of color. Everywhere, homes are painted yellow, pink, blue, turquoise, orange, green, and any other color you can imagine.

deWaterkant
by Rayna Gillman,
24½″ × 41½″, 2016

Photo by Rayna Gillman

Most people tell me they see windows when they look at *deWaterkant* (previous page). I see a tenement, but my inspiration was the pattern on a piece of pottery in a Cape Town gallery (at right).

I couldn't bring the piece home with me, but I have the image. And at some level, both Cape Town's pottery and its buildings conspired to make this piece what it is.

WHAT INSPIRES YOU?

As you have seen, inspiration and improvisation are not mutually exclusive. The artists in this book were all inspired by *something*, and none of them used a pattern or a detailed plan. Some started with an idea; others just began piecing without anything in mind. Either way, the journey is always an adventure.

What's next for you? If you find yourself staring into space, wondering where your next inspiration is hiding, I hope the next chapter will help you find it.

Artist unknown

Photo by Rayna Gillman

JUMP-START YOUR MUSE

Whether you are conscious of it or not, you are influenced by your life, your surroundings, your emotions, your memories, a sound, a color, a line, a shape, a pattern, a scrap of cloth, a word … the list goes on. Here are some suggestions that can help you mine these influences.

observe your surroundings

Chances are, you take your smartphone with you wherever you go. Look around you and use the camera to take photos of everything that intrigues, appeals to, amuses, or moves you, whether it is in nature, on the street, or even in your own home.

look at art

Galleries and museums are treasure troves of ideas. Ask about photo policies, and if you can take a picture with your smartphone, do it. Could the shape of this sculpture have subliminally influenced some of the kite shapes in my work?

Folded Plywood 2
by Harry Roseman,
43¾˝ wide × 72˝ high × ¾˝ deep, 2011

Photo by Rayna Gillman

make a file of images

Do you take lots of photos of one thing? Trees? Buildings? Leaves? Windows? People? You may also keep a notebook with magazine images that attract you. Go through your photos and ask yourself these questions:

How do the images make me feel?

Some photos may evoke a visceral response. These may find their way into your work in a way that will probably not resemble the original scenes depicted but will reflect your feelings.

This work expressed the loneliness I felt late one night in a nearly empty subway car.

Here is the photo that inspired that piece.

View from the Uptown Express by Rayna Gillman, 29″ × 36″, 2016

Photo by Rayna Gillman

Uptown express train; inspiration for *View from the Uptown Express*

Photo by Rayna Gillman

Is there a line or a shape that speaks to me?

Is there is a line or shape that speaks to you? Use that line as a starting point. This cherry tree has a number of lines you can begin with. Find one, sketch it, extend it, and see where it takes you. Then see if there is another shape that inspires you and use it to jump-start a piece. If you sketch an idea, keep it to a minimum: Leave out the details and focus on the outline.

Look at your photos for shapes that appear and reappear. Here's one image of an abandoned dwelling from my inspiration file.

Abandoned dwelling, Fort Hancock, New Jersey

Photo by Rayna Gillman

A variety of window shapes have appeared in my improv works over the years.

Night Windows by Rayna Gillman, 12″ × 12″, 2012

The shape appears—unbidden—in my modern pieces as well, even though I do not intend them to represent windows.

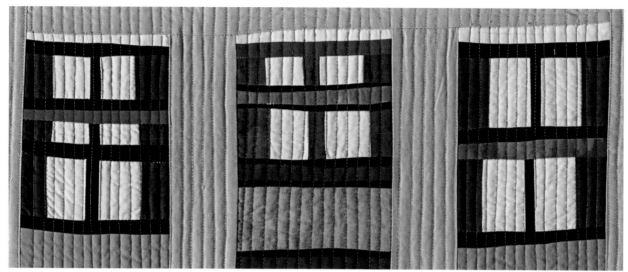

Detail of *deWaterkant* (page 76)

Here are more photos from my files. I see that parallel lines are evidently embedded in my subconscious because they appear in my work so frequently.

Strata by Rayna Gillman, 42″ × 29″, 2009

Spring Rain by Rayna Gillman, 12″ × 12″, 2011

Photo by Rayna Gillman

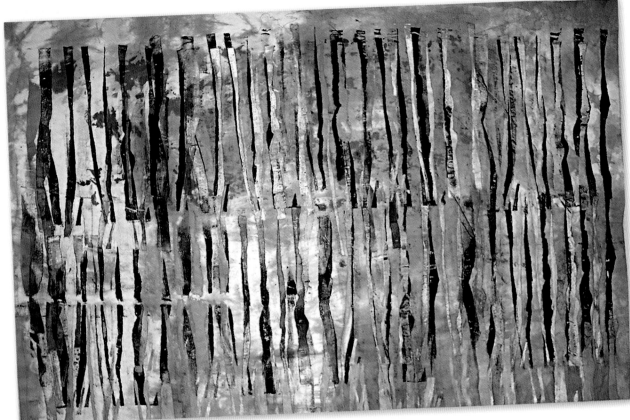

Element by Rayna Gillman, 40″ × 25″, 2009

Photo by Rayna Gillman

This is one of the quilts that got me into strips and stripes.

TAKE THE COLOR CHALLENGE

Color has power. It's the first thing you notice, and you often have an emotional response to it. You may use certain combinations over and over again because you are comfortable with them. But too much repetition can be boring. How can you get out of the rut and let color give you a creative fresh start?

TIP: Use solids for these explorations so you are not distracted by pattern.

color switcheroo

Switch out one color for another of the same or similar value and make a simple block to see how it works. Audition one color at a time; then pick a combination and use it.

For example, blue, pink, and purple are easy to use together because they are all from the same side of the color wheel.

If you trade the pink for an unexpected orangey red, the combination is more interesting.

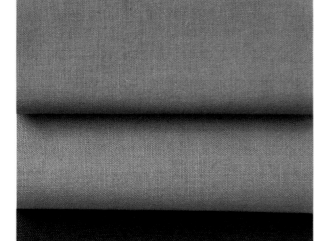

A sweet combination

A little spicier

keep your eyes open

Great places to look for unexpected color pairings that work:

Clothing (both men's and women's) shop windows

Photo by Rayna Gillman

Home furnishings stores, home decor magazines, and websites

This carpet I saw in a Paris shop is a perfect example of unexpected, inspiring color combinations.

Photo by Rayna Gillman

Art—in person, online, or in publications

Whether sculptures (see Folded Plywood 2, page 78), paintings, stained glass, graphics, or any other medium, inspiration can be found wherever you are.

Your surroundings

The New York scene one rainy night inspired the palette here. I would not normally have thought to use these colors together, but there they were, in front of me. Life inspires art!

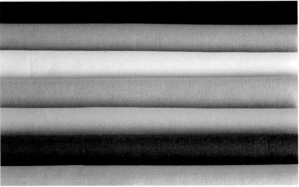

Photos by Rayna Gillman

These two men in the London Underground wore remarkably similar colors, although I am sure they did not choose their outfits together.

Photo by Rayna Gillman

- -

Below is a hotel carpet, a continent away, in a similar palette to the men in the Underground, but it is less successful—too many shades of beige with no contrast. The mustard adds nothing to the combination, since it is so close to the light beige in value that it disappears. Almost any accent color in a medium value would help, as would a solid ground of the darker beige.

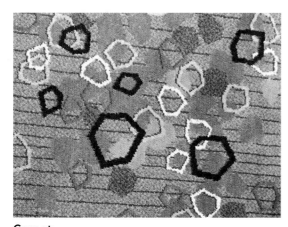

Carpet
Photo by Rayna Gillman

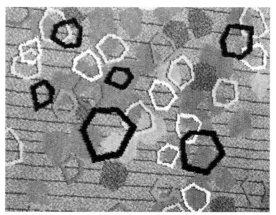

Photo of the carpet converted to black and white, showing how similar in value the colors are overall
Photo by Rayna Gillman

Keep value in mind when you choose your colors.

use your lonely crayon

Which crayon remained unused in the box when you were a child? Chances are you still don't use much of that color; maybe you dislike it or simply don't know how to use it. Try this.

1 Dive into your color box.

If you have watercolor crayons or paints, which ones are still unused? Take them out and mine your stash for similar colors.

2 Pull out the lonely color and a second color you rarely use.

You don't have to love them, but no color stands alone, and you might be surprised at how effective they can be together.

3 Find another color that works with both of them.

Pay attention to value so there is contrast. When you add a third color, magic can happen.

4 Play on your design wall.

Keep an open mind, keep experimenting, and feel free to add a fourth color. Use these colors with white or light gray, which can make them pop, tone them down, or make them look fresh and modern.

revisit your photos

Look for color combinations you may have missed while you were focused on line, shape, and other elements. Something may inspire you.

Here are photos I took in Cape Town, where the appliances are as colorful as the buildings. Both of these are unusual combinations that would look great in a modern quilt. Would you have thought of using black, orange, and pale blue together?

I intend to play with this combination one of these days.

Photo by Rayna Gillman

Photo by Rayna Gillman

START WITH A WORD

Words are just as powerful as images, and they often elicit interesting and unexpected associations. Open a book to any page and without looking, put your finger on a word. That can be a good starting point for free association that will give you an idea for a quilt. There are also random word generators online that will give you a list of adjectives and/or nouns.

1. Make or find a list of nouns and/or adjectives.

2. Pick a word that appeals to you and use it to get started. For example, *prickly* or *wavy* might conjure up a line or a shape you can use in your quilt.

3. Or, pick a word at random and free-associate to see where the word takes you.

Here are some adjectives and nouns to get you started.

Adjectives	Nouns
red	triangle
spiky	chair
long	square
soft	fence
bright	cabinet
orange	square

MAKE A MIND MAP

A mind map is a visual thinking tool—a way to jump-start creativity by putting down your thoughts and free associations like branches of a tree, rather than in list form. All you need is a piece of blank paper and something to write with.

1. Pick a word and place it in the middle of the paper.

2. Draw a line and write the first word that comes into your mind.

3. Branch out from there. Do not censor yourself. Stop after 2 or 3 minutes or when you find yourself stopping to think.

4. Pick a word association that resonates with you and use that to spark your next quilt idea.

This is a mind map that I drew. Yours will look different because nobody approaches it the same way. If you do an online search for mind maps, you will find a lot of information. But it is best to keep it simple.

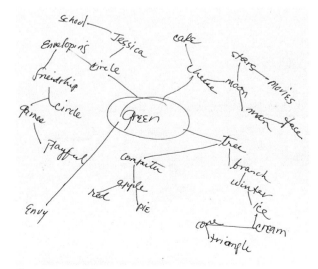

Photo by Rayna Gillman

For me, the spark was the "circle" association—and I see that it came up twice and sparked *Green Circle*, which I made 35 years ago when my daughter was in elementary school. If I were to make it today based on the same words, it would be a very different quilt.

Green Circle by Rayna Gillman, 18″ × 18″, 1982
Photo by Rayna Gillman

If you are stuck, try one of these methods to get you started with your next no-pattern quilt. You can go back to these exercises again and again and discover something new every time. Inspiration is everywhere. No matter where you find it, you can use it to make an original quilt with a modern look. Keep your eyes open and enjoy the journey!

QUESTIONS AND ANSWERS

In nearly every workshop, students invariably ask certain questions about my work. I'd like to share some of them with you—along with my answers and some illustrations.

Q How do you quilt your pieces?

A: Straight lines. They are easy (although not necessarily quick), and I believe they lend themselves beautifully to the modern quilt aesthetic. They are minimalist and simple, and I find they add texture without overwhelming the color and design of the quilts.

Q Your work isn't generally very big, is it?

A: True. I think the largest quilt I've made has been around 48″ × 48″. My quilts tell me when they are done, and most seem to stop in the 25″–40″ range. I also love 10″ × 10″ or 12″ × 12″ sizes, which I mount on gallery-wrap canvas so they don't look like oversized potholders. Except for one quilt that's featured in this book (*Strings in Half-Time*, pages 41 and 46), I stopped making bed quilts more than 25 years ago.

Q How do you know when a piece is done?

There are really two answers to this question.

A #1: *You don't always know.*
If you are working without a pattern or a preconceived size, it's not always clear whether the piece on your wall is ready to be put together. Maybe it needs more, maybe less. When in doubt, try the following:

- Let it sit for a day or three.

- Ask another artist or two—whose eye(s), work, and opinion(s) you respect—for feedback.

- Let it sit for another day.

- If you are really stuck, take everything down and start putting the pieces back one at a time. This never fails to improve the piece.

A #2: *You just know.*
This is a combination of instinct, experience, and listening to the work on the wall. It will tell you, your eye will tell you, and your instincts will tell you. Follow your instincts; if it feels right, it is done.

A CAUTIONARY TALE

Remember those blocks made with the leftover triangles? (Look back at No-Pattern Paper Piecing, page 57.)

Here's what happens when you don't follow your instincts. When I had enough blocks for a mini quilt, I arranged them in an alternate grid. The layout felt static, but I had sewn together some houses from the extra triangles and thought they would add some life to the piece.

I increased the size of the turquoise background to add space and played with the design, but nothing made me think, "Stick a fork in it—it's done." However, I was impatient to move on, and although something about the piece bothered me I decided it was "good enough." Not everything has to be a masterpiece, and after all, it was an experiment. I was committed to finishing it, so I kept going.

The quilting didn't improve it, but the colors were bright and I thought some child might like it on her wall. Then, a surprise! As I rotated the quilt to sew down the facing, I realized *I had forgotten to follow my own advice to look at the quilt in all directions.* As soon as I changed the orientation, in any direction, the quilt changed from static to dynamic and took on new life.

The quilt was rescued by a change in direction, but had I let it sit for a day or two, a better solution might have come to me. Lesson learned: *Don't be in a hurry to finish something if it doesn't feel right. Banish that little voice of reason in your head and let the piece rest.*

Turned upside down, the sky was falling!

Sideways, they were off to the races. Either way, there was movement.

Q Some of your early quilts are sort of free-motion quilted. Why did you switch?

A: Ha ha! "Sort of" hits the nail on the head. I flunked every free-motion class I ever took.

My stitches went from long to short and were messy. I dreaded quilting and frequently left the quilts for months before I quilted them. I finally decided my quilts were not about the stitch.

An aside ... As I practiced quilting the negative space in *Go Fly a Kite* (page 47), I knew I would have neither the time nor the patience to do a whole quilt.

So for the first time, I handed two quilts over to a professional. Because longarm quilters typically use complicated, computer-driven patterns and I wanted straight lines, this quilt had to be custom quilted. I blessed it and released it, but I was nervous because it was out of my control.

I am very happy with the way it turned out. In keeping with the improv nature of the quilt, Diane varied the quilting to work with

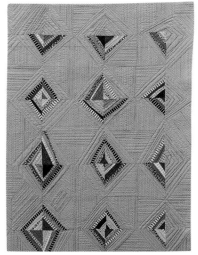

My practice piece with its bad quilting

the irregular spaces. Best of all, she quilted ghost kites into the space at the edges so it would not look like a border. Looks great!

Detail of improv quilting for the improv quilt *Go Fly a Kite* (page 47)

Q *How do you finish your quilts? I don't see a binding.*

A: I face my quilts. This gives a sleeker and more modern look to the pieces. I've been facing my quilts since 2000. It is a similar process to binding, except less bulky because it's a single layer, not double. It's also turned completely to the back so you don't see it. Best of all, you don't need mitered corners!

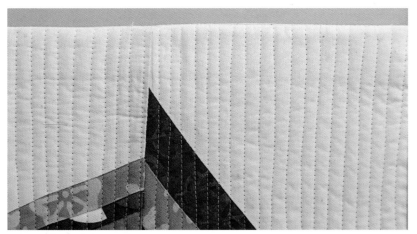

Front edge of the quilt

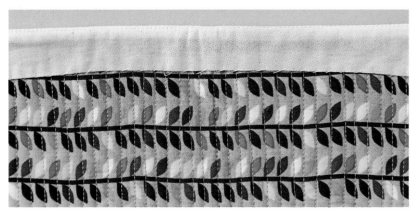

Back edge of the quilt

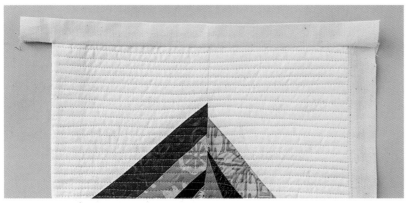

This is a piece in process. The left-hand side has the finished edge. (Refer to Finishing with a Facing, next page.}

FINISHING WITH A FACING

1. Trim the batting back ¼″ on all sides, if possible. At the very least, trim the corners of the batting back. This eliminates bulk when the finished corners come together.

2. Cut facing strips anywhere from 1¼″ to 2″ wide, depending on the size of the quilt.

3. Turn under ¼″ on one long edge of the facing strip and press. *Optional:* Machine stitch the edge.

4. Sew facing strips to the raw edges of the quilt on opposite sides.

The turned-under edge and facing sewn to the quilt's raw edge

5. Trim the strips so they are even with the remaining raw edges of the quilt.

6. Press and understitch. This will help the strips lie flat when you turn them to the back.

Trimmed and understitched facing strip

7. Turn the strip to the back, press, and hand stitch down.

8. Cut 2 more strips about 1″ longer than the finished edges of the quilt and repeat on the other sides. Do not trim these strips.

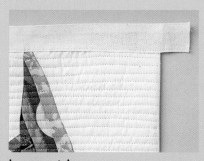

Longer strips

9. Fold the overlapping ends to the back so the folds are even with the finished edge.

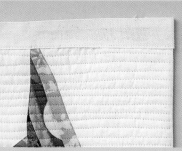

Strip folded in

10. Turn to the back and hand stitch to the back of the quilt.

Finished corner

So now you are there: You've finished the quilt and now have to add a sleeve if it is going on the wall. But you already know how to do that.

If you have any questions I haven't covered here, please email me and ask. I have no secrets.

Remember to experiment as you make quilts with a modern sensibility. You'll have fun, you'll make discoveries, and when you work without a pattern your quilt will reflect you. Enjoy the process and the result will take care of itself!

Rayna Gillman made her first quilt when, as a young mother, she found a quilting class at the local art museum. The bicentennial and the quilting explosion had not yet happened and she didn't know anyone who quilted. Except for that first class, she has been self-taught.

Although she started with traditional quilts, she eventually began asking herself "What if … ?" Knowing she had nothing to lose, she experimented and found her own way of doing things. She put the ruler aside and cut freehand. She sliced up pieces she was not happy with and made them into something fresh. She printed her own fabrics and combined them with fabrics in her stash. Above all, she improvised, and for nearly two decades she has been teaching others how to develop their own abilities to improvise and create free-form quilts.

Now she brings her improvisational way of working and her intuitive sense of color to the world of modern quilts. She invites you to continue the journey with her, combining free-form with modern—a perfect fit!

You can find Rayna at her website (**studio78.net**), on her blog (**studio78.net/blog**), on Facebook (**/rayna.gillman**), and on Instagram (**@rayna_gillman**).

Also by Rayna Gillman:

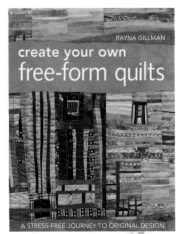

RESOURCES FOR ETHNIC FABRICS

ABORIGINAL AUSTRALIAN AND AFRICAN FABRICS

Artistic Artifacts   artisticartifacts.com

INDIAN AND MALAYSIAN BATIKS

Handloom Batik   handloombatik.com

AFRICAN FABRICS

More Love Mama   morelovemama.net

The African Fabric Shop   africanfabric.co.uk

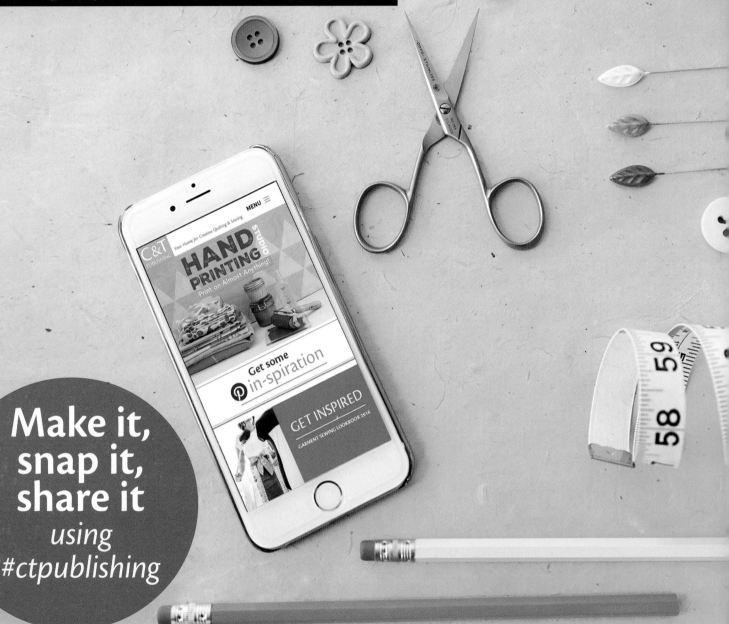

Want even more creative content?